Daddys Master

Roxanne Veils

Copyright © 2024 by Roxanne Veils

All rights reserved.

No portion of this book may be reproduced in any form without written permission from the publisher or author, except as permitted by U.S. copyright law.

Contents

1. Chapter one — 1
2. Chapter two — 4
3. chapter three — 8
4. chapter four — 11
5. chapter five — 14
6. chapter six — 16
7. chapter seven — 20
8. chapter eight — 23
9. chapter nine — 25
10. Chapter ten — 28
11. chapter eleven — 31
12. chapter twelve — 34
13. Chapter thirteen — 36
14. Chapter fourteen — 40
15. chapter fifteen — 45

16.	Chapter sixteen	47
17.	chapter seventeen	54
18.	Chapter eighteen	58
19.	Chapter nineteen	63
20.	Chapter Twenty	68
21.	chapter twenty two	75
22.	Chapter Twenty one	78
23.	chapter twenty three	81
24.	Chapter twenty four	84
25.	chapter twenty five	89
26.	chapter twenty six	94
27.	Chapter Twenty seven	99
28.	Chapter twenty eight	102
29.	Chapter twenty nine	104
30.	chapter thirty	112

Chapter one

My life wasn't all sunshine and rainbows like in my dreams,it was... let's just say unpleasant. I had no friends and no boyfriend. I swear at college called me an ice queen. Not saying that I'm not familiar with that name.

When my parents told me that I got to start growing up,I thought maybe i had to start doing my house chores twice as hard. But no. They were telling me to move the fuck out nicely.

They bought me a car,gave me money to sustain myself for a while and helped me pack up the next day. It has been two years since I spoke to them . The only communication I got from them was a flimsy letter saying that I was adopted. That didn't even suprise me.

I didn't have any of their feature like long brown hair or their trademark thin waists. I was on the chubby side. Big brown eyes and let's not begin about the tangled mess on my head. Right now said tangled mess swallowed my pencil and the class is boring as fuck. I like Mrs Long but I'd rather be in the library, reading a steamy book about Alpha males and their mate.

"Earth to Vivian," Mrs Long said. I stopped searching for my pencil and gave her my attention. Everyone was looking at me. That didn't sit well with my insecurities. "Sorry," I said silently bagging the floor to open up and swallow me. She continued and they stopped staring. Except one person.

Sir.

It's an unusual name but he own it like no body's business. I stared back at him and lost interest in what Mrs Long was talking about. I refuse to back down . He smirked and gave Mrs Long his attention. I took a deep breath and tried to focus. Thirty more minutes to go. Great.

~•~

My shift was close to end and I couldn't wait to get home and crash. I so tired,I could just sleep on the shiny floor. Working for Mr Smith at the Dungeon was quite an experience. My social skills have improved and the pay here is awesome.

It was also my favourite job between the working here and at the Mrs Halls. That place is just...so close to the college. All the bullies go there for lunch and make my life hell. I've learnt how to ignore their comments and suffer inside. That's not healthy but,oh well.

"Vivian,"Nora called." Booth six,"she said handing me the drinks. I gave her a smile before going to deliver the drinks. I almost Spillers the drinks when I saw who was sitting in the booth. Sir and another man. He smirked and whispered something to the other man.

They both stared at me and I think they were checking me out. I lowered my eyes and put the drink on the table. "Enjoy your evening," I said. Before I could walk away,Sir spoke.

"Don't you have manners, Vivian." His deep voice was like music to my ears. I called listen to him talk and never get tired. "No," I said before scurrying away.

That night, my dreams consisted of Sir and his marvelous voice doing forbidden things to my body.

Chapter two

If there's a part I hate more about my life, that part would be my annoying alarm clock. I can't stand the small fucker yet I still kip it. Last night's shift felt longer than normal and serving Sir didn't help. I swear I never got out of the bar that fast.

My legs tangle some more into my sheets when I've finally decided to get up. I yelp and fall ungraciously to the floor. Fuck. I slowly get up and rub my painful limbs. Fucking get up and walk it out, I hear my mom's voice in my head. My left ass cheek. I scowl at the annoying voice in my head. Get out, I yell at it.

Take a shower and dress for the day. Black tights and a black t-shirt with a skull bleeding silver liquid. How lady like. Cringe . I look nothing like a lady. The girls at school drove that message home perfectly. Sluts. I give myself another once over and decided that they must go fuck themselves for all I care.

When I got to school, the first people I saw was Leah and her friends. I don't really know what I've done to this girls but they despise my guts. One time, they locked me in the bathroom. I had a test on that day. I got so mad that I wrote the test crying. I'll never forget how people started avoiding me.

Waiting, waiting and waiting in my car so I could avoid interecting with them. Someone banged on my window and I flinched. It was Sir. I lowered the window and stared at him."Why are you still in your car?" He asked. I continued staring at him in shock.

Why was he talking to me? My door opened and he pulled me out." Wait," I told him. I got back in and collected my phone and books. He took my bag and started walking which forced me to scurry behind him like a mouse chasing cheese.

"You didn't answer me," he said when I cought up to him. "Don't make me repeat myself, Vivian." Wait. Sir knows my name. Fucking Sir,the most popular guy knows my name. I tried to say something but my throat just refused to co-operate. I pointed at Leah and her friends.

He looked at them and a scary look crossed his face before it was replaced by a smirk. "Yo Sir,what are you doing with the fat girl," Leah asked, running towards us. No. No. No. No. Floor please open and swallow me. "I was waiting for you," she continued, putting her devils hand on his chest.

"Well," Sir said, loudly enough for everyone to hear. " This beautiful,sexy gift from God is...my girlfriend." A paper clip fell. The shock on everyone's eyes was... priceless but mine was...damn. Like, what the fuck just happened?

He got closer to me and kissed my forehead before towards Mr Lion's class. Eyes wide,throat dry, heart attacking my chest. I fell into step with him and he put his muscular arm around my shoulder. God. Why am I so short. I look like a dwarf compared to this greek god.

~•~

After school, I tried to avoid everyone as always and get to work before my shift begun. I don't have to work to the bar tonight. During class,I felt everyone's curious eyes on me. Did that sit well with my insecurities? No. It did not.

I didn't see Sir during break so I thought he left school early. Courtesy to my bad luck,a wall of muscles appeared infront of me from no where. I closed my eyes and cursed my bad luck.

"That pretty mouth wasn't made for such a bad word," he said in a deep voice that did things to my insides.

I took a deep breath and looked up at him. "Hello, Sir," I said. He closed his eyes and groaned. "I like the way my name sounds from your lovely voice. It's so sweet and smooth I could listen to you scream it while I rail you from behind," he said. That made my clit instantly throb. I clenched my inner walls to get rid of the sensation. That made everything worse.

He smirked before kissing my forehead and whispering,"See you later," in my ear. I stood there not knowing what to do after he left. I stared at his back and admired his fine ass before he disappeared. I shook myself and hurried to my car.

I got to Mrs Halls's a little bit later than I wanted to be. I found Harley cleaning the tables and waved at her. I wore my uniform and started doing my job. Customer's, mainly the people from my college started filling in and occupying the tables.

Harley went and took their orders. Mrs Halls handed me the tray with their food and I took a few breaths before getting to work. Here goes nothing. All the boys have me weird looks and the girls glared at me. Okay, the fuck is going on.

The bell at the door ringed, signalling another customer's arrival. Warm hards landed on my hips and soft lips came down on my neck.

Sir.

chapter three

"Stop, everyone is looking," I whispered. He just continued showering my neck with kisses. My head tilted on its own to give him more access. Damn. This feels good.

I heard him chuckle before whispering," I don't care. They could watch me devour your pussy right here and now and I still won't give two fucks". Melt.

" I got work to do, Sir," I whispered back. I was grinning. Why was I grinning? Because secretly you want this man to do all those dirty things to you. Treacherous mind. Treacherous body.

"I want to spend time with my girlfriend. Is that too much to ask," he said. Fuck. Almost forgot about that.

"I'm not your girlfriend,Sir," I whispered. He tightened his hold on my hips and I whimpered. God. What is this man doing to my body.

"You think so?"he asked. I nodded. " You so damn wrong Vivian. You are mine but I'll wait for you to get that into that pretty head of yours. I'm one patient man," he said with a smirk on his face. He kissed my forehead before joining his friends close to the counter.

Great.

~•~

My shift at Mrs Halls felt so goddamned long. Sir kept on staring at me throughout his lunch with his friends. At least they didn't bother me so that's something I'm grateful for.

I found myself smiling as I took a bath. Do I want him to be my boyfriend? I giggled at that question. Something about Sir makes me wanna get on my knees and stay there.

I finished bathing and just layed on my bed in my fluffy towel. My thoughts revolved around Sir ."You messing with my head Mr," I whispered to the silence in my apartment.

I let my towel fall and layed back on my pillows. My hand travelled south. I closed my eyes and drew circles on my clit as I thought about everything Sir could do to me.

The circle got smaller and faster as I head him say what he said to me at Mrs Halls. I moaned his name in pleasure as I inserted a finger inside me and put more pressure on my clit.

My release left me wanting more. Craving more. Craving him. I got under the sheets and slept as soon as my head touched the pillow.

~•~

" This that hot girl bummer anthem..." Took the small offending device and answered without checking the caller ID. "Hello," I whispered. I hope you woke me up for a good reason.

"Vivian," someone rasped. This voice sounded familiar. Sir? "Sir?" I said, fully waking up. "You sound so sexy when you just woke up,"he said. Damn. You are the one who sounds sexy.

"What do you want?" I asked. I looked at the time and saw that it was nine p.m. " Is that the proper way to talk to your man?" he asked. I groaned and stared at my ceiling.

" Since you aren't my boyfriend, it is the proper way to talk to you," I said, grinning at my smart ass reply. "Is that so,baby girl?" He said. "Yes," I said. "That smart mouth of yours deserves to be fucked," he said. His voice lowering dangerously.

My smile vanished instantly. Why does he have to say things like that. " Okay Mr. Let's pretend you didn't say that,Kay. Now let me go back to sleep before I murder you with my boobs in your sleep," I said before disconnecting the call. Cringe.

Kill. Me. Now

chapter four

My thoughts before I sleep were of Sir and all the dirty things he said he'd do to me. My hand travelled south, seeking the little bundle of nerves hidden by my folds. My other hand followed it to open them so I can relieve myself of the agonising sensation deep inside me.

A small moan escaped my lips when my wet fingers came into contact with my clit. Damn. I wonder how It would feel if he was the one doing this to me.

The circulation on my clit got smaller and the added pressure made me vocalise my pleasure louder. The pressure built higher and higher and higher.

This orgasm felt like a mini rainbow. Light colours and small but beautiful and sweet. So, so sweet.

I couldn't wait for it to be morning already. Some sadistic part of me couldn't wait to see Sir. I wonder what he'll say...or do. As I finished eating my mediocre breakfast, took what I'd need for the day and left my apartment.

Today felt exciting and... dangerous. Terrible combination if you ask me but oh well.

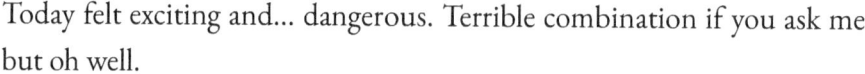

I expected to find him glaring at my favourite parking spot but what I saw tore my heart. I wasn't mentally prepared for the show in front of me. Sir was desplayig his gorgeous smile at Leah and her lapdogs .

For a moment I was taken aback by it. And then the stupid whore clawed at his chest with her demonic nails. Okay,they are pretty but the owner makes them look like claws.

Breath Vivian, breath.

I stepped out of my car but had to lean in and collect my stuff. I felt a hand on my hips. Caressing so damn slow that it made me shiver.

" I wonder how this ass would look glowing red,bite marks and several hand prints," he said. Sir.

"Aren't we glad that it's one of the things you'll die without experiencing," I said. I absolutely loved and hated my moments of confidence. All they ever do is get me in trouble .

"That mouth baby girl," he said, tightening his hold on my hips. A silent moan escaped my lips. He chuckled. I took a deep breath to try and calm my nerves and bravely said, " Give a girl some space, Sir. I got a class to get to."

Once I was upright, a had was on my throat. "You sure are such a brat, Vivian and brats... let's just say they get what they ask for. I suggest you drop the attitude and be a good girl for me," he said running his nose along my sensitive neck.

His hold on my neck tightened a little. A mischievous grin split my face before I moved closer to his ear. If he could play this game, I'll also play along. What I did dug my grave so deep, I wouldn't be able to see the surface even if I tried.

I saw myself lick the shell of his earlobe before I whispered, "Make me."

His hand dropped beside him which gave an escape window. My large globes came into contact with his hard chest.

All he did was stare at me in shock or something along those lines. His beautiful eyes never left me, not even once. I turned on my heels and put a little spice into my steps.

When I was a good distance away from him, I broke into a sprint. The smile on my face was too big and freaking painful.

I'm fucked

chapter five

Avoiding Sir and the whore turned out to be one heck of a chore. Now I'm damn hungry due to avoiding the cafeteria. Sir was guarding the cafeteria entrance like a dog. An angry dog. He looked so hot all angry and all.

I was the first one to exist the school building when classes were over. When I entered my car, all I thought about was food and going somewhere were Sir can not access me. The figure behind my car was not clear until I almost ran him over.

Can a person look that bloodthirsty and hot at the same time? It should be illegal. Do I have a danger fetish or something? I wondered. He just stood there and glared at me. Stupid, stupid, stupid.

I should have never got that close to him. I should have never played along with his stupid seduction games. He slowly made his way around my car to my door. Each step he took made me wanna hide in my bag. What a mouse, I head Leah's voice.

I slowly raised my head from my hands...Sir wasn't behind my car anymore. The loud knock on my window made me jump and scream. He's still here. Fuck.

" Get out," he said calmly. That scared the shit out of me even more. A calm Sir is a dangerous Sir. I took my sweet ass time unlocking my old car and opened it so slow even a sloth seemed fast.

Sir pulled it open with so much force that it almost broke. I stepped out of my car and stepped aside so I don't get hurt when he banged it close. He got so close to me I could feel his minty breath on my lips.

He caged me against my car while he stared straight into my eyes. "Look at me," he commanded. I kept looking at his beautiful chest. Nice chest. I would have liked to fantasize about it from afar but no . My big mouth and slutty behaviour had to get his attention.

"Don't make me repeat myself, Vivian," he said. I slowly looked at him and found his beautiful, lustful eyes glaring at me. "No one has ever in my life gathered the ovaries to do what you did today. Do you know how hard it is to concentrate in class with a raging hard on, Vivian. Do you?" He said, trailing his large hands on my hips.

"Answer me," he growled. I shook my head frantically. I really am a mouse."Words Vivian. I expect you to use them," he said, tightening his hold on me. " No, Sir," I said. He took deep breath before getting close to my ear.

" Of cause you don't and that's why you are going to pay for it. From now on,I declare you my girlfriend. That's right,mine. That's your punishment for giving me a hard on that refuses to go away." Well that's not a bad thing,is it. I can do that.

Then I sold my soul to the devil with a single," Okay."

Idiot

chapter six

~Sir~

I've finally got her. The most beautiful, sweetest girl in college and she's my girlfriend. I wonder how Master is going to react to this. He's the one who tasked me to make Vivian my submissive after all.

Yesterday she gave me the worst hard on on earth. Reminds me of Master and how he can rail me as punishment for teasing him in the morning before an important meeting. Damn that man can fuck.

My phone vibrates from the coffee table and I lazily grab it. It's Master. "Hey kitten. I'm almost home," he said. That made my pants get hard instantly. "And," I ask. "Under your pillow, there is a card. Do as it says," he said in a deep tone. I almost moaned.

"Okay, see you then." I went straight to our room and retrieved the card under my pillow. Strip Kneel on Master's side of the bed Blindfold on Cock ring on Don't move until Master tells you to

I was already hard for him but the thought of having Vivian here. Getting her pussy ready for Master to destroy. Mmm, that would be so hot. Of cause he won't be the only one claiming her.

I slowly get rid of my clothes and wait for Master to come play with me. The cock ring on my dick teases me in the lowest beautiful way.

I imagine Vivian's mouth around it. Sucking my dick like her life depended on it. Looking at me with those big, beautiful eyes of hers. Begging me to grace her pussy with my touch. Mmmm.

I heard the front door close as Master made his way to our room. I didn't close the door but I couldn't actually see anything with the black silk over my eyes. " Kitten," Master whispered .

"Yes Master," I said. I'm sure his beautiful eyes are on my erect cock. That made me whisper a moan. "Fuck, aren't you Master's sexy pet," he said. I licked the side of his neck. Master inhaled and grabbed my cock.

"Do you want Master's dick in your mouth or in your ass," he asked. I sucked on his neck harder to leave a mark. He squeezed my dick and increased the speed. My lips left his neck and I moaned in his ear.

"Don't cum," he growled when I whined that I'm close. If I cummed without permission, he'd make me cum five times as a punishment . "Yes Kitten, that's it. Moan for Master. Let the neighbours know my name." He said. This man wants to kill me.

"Master...fuck. Please Master...I can't hold it in anymore. Please...Fuck let me cum Master," I screamed. I really don't want to be punished but this man is...,"Cum for Master,Kitten," he growled, nipping at my ear.

Ribbon after ribbon after ribbon of cum dirtied the floor as Master kept on milking me. He didn't stop though. He increased the vibration on the cock ring and continued jerking me until I was a crying mess on the floor. Fuck. I knew he'd do this.

"Good boy,"he purred as he got ready to fuck my ass until I couldn't walk.

~•~

~Vivian~

It has been four days since Sir declared me as his girlfriend. I don't want to seem desparate but the amount of times I waited for his call or message are a bit much. A bit.

It was three am when I received a call. My sleepy ass answered the call without checking the caller id again. "Why are you answering calls at...three," he asked. Fucking Sir. I rubbed my eyes. "Why are you making calls at three?" I retorted.

He chuckled . " You begging to be punished princess?" He asked. How am I begging to be punished? This man is crazy. "So you woke me up at three in the morning just to tell me that I'm begging to be punished," I asked.

Silence. Oh hell no. "Fucking call me when you have something serious to talk about and call me at reasonable hours... like two days ago..." The call was disconnected.

Asshole

I snuggled deeper into my covers and prepared to get back to sleep. A loud banging on my door made me jump and fall off my bed. Dammit.

Who the fuck knocks like that? At this time of the morning? Whoever they are, they are dead meat. Dead.

As I get up and stomp my way to the door, the tangled sheets on my feet deliver me to the cold floor again. I spew a string of curses while I untangle my self.

The banging at my door continues, waking very tired and angry neighbours in the process. I restart my angry stomps to my door and come face to face with an angry Sir.

"Morning princess."

chapter seven

In case I don't survive this Lord, know that I deserve to be in heaven. Among good angels and not to burn in hell...

"What are you looking at," he asked. I just continued staring at the ceiling, pleading with God to allotw me to be one of his angels."Don't make me ask again Princess," he repeated,in a low tone.

Amen! I can die in piece now.

I sighed before giving him my tired stare. I rolled my eyes at him before I made my way to the kitchen leaving the door open. I started on my tea and heated three cookies from Mrs Halls. She bakes the best chocolate chip cookies.

"Aren't you going to ask me if I want a cup?" Sir asked while locking my door. I dramatically sighed and raised an eyebrow at him. I'm not talking to him. I'll only make him angrier. "You clearly have no manners, Princess."

I shrugged. He slowly made his way behind me while I was reaching for the sugar container. I felt strong hands on my thinly clad hips. Soft lips trailed wet kisses on my neck while I suppressed the moans that threatened to escape my lips.

"Bend over," he whispered. I shook my head. I head him chuckle. "You dare to disobey me, Princess?" He said. His big hands cupping my globes and squeezing hard. Eliciting a breathy moan out of me.

" I'm going to repeat myself for the last time, Princess. Bend fucking over," he growled. I complied. His hands trailed from my stomach to my hips again.

"Ten spanks and you are going to count. Don't make a mistake Princess, I'd hate to start again,"he said in a low tone.

~•~

~Sir~

I wonder what my intentions were when I got in my car and drove straight to her building. What I didn't expect is bending my Princess over her own furniture.

"Don't forget to count baby girl," I said. Feeling the smooth curve of her ass. Fucking beautiful . She gasped as my hand made contact with her left ass cheek. "Count!" I growled. "One," she whispered.

Three spanks followed the first one. "Two, three, four," she gasped out. Her whimpers made me so hard. "This material is too thin for my baby. Where you expecting me baby girl?" I asked.

She shook her head." Is that so, Princess," I said, preparing to deliver four spanks to her gorgeous ass. "Five...Six...Sir I...Seven. Oh God, Sir st... Eight. Ahh," she screamed. Fuck. Ain't that music to my ears.

"This is going to hurt baby girl. A lot worse than the ones you already received. Or you might just end up liking it like a good pain slut." I watched in excitement when she tried to clench her thighs. Damn.

I pressed down on her clit over her panties. The moans that escaped her kissable lips gave way to a groan from me. Master is going to enjoy edging you. You'll die of orgasms from him and I'll bury my cock in your wet heat while you suck his cock.

My hand landed on her pussy so fast that she screamed in pleasure. The last spank had her cumming in her underwear and shaking. "Good girl," I praised her as she rode the last waves of her orgasm.

I turned off the stove and picked my Princess up. I layed her down on her couch and sat next to her. "I expect you to call me by my name in public and Daddy behind closed doors. Or anywhere I might feel like taking what's mine from you. You okay with that."

She nodded,too tired to utter a word or move,I presume. That made me grin with pride. "Also, remember to be a good girl,my good girl at all times or suffer consequences similar to this one but worse." She nodded again.

I kissed her firstly on the cheeks and then her forehead. "Where's your bedroom," I ask as I picked her up again. She directed me with her finger. I got to her room and went straight to her bed.

I undressed her and put her in a loose t-shirt. I got in beside her and dozed off to her soft breathing and a scent that is all her.

chapter eight

Warning:short chapterSorry (口•口•)

BeepBeepBeepBeep

Ahggg. Somebody make it stop. Please. I unconsciously slam a fist on my alarm clock snuggle against the warm body under me.

WaitWhy am I on top of a warm body?

Without opening my eyes,I feel my way up to the sculptured body and wiggle a little. "Stop." I froze. Why is he still here and why am I on top of him?

Stupid. Stupid. Stupid. "Morning, Princess," he said. Damn that voice sounds like dripping honey. His hands griped my ass and he moved his hips in a way that made feel his morning wood. That feels so... good.

"Mmmm, Princess,"he groaned against my head. And my horny ass moaned. He chuckled and halted his movements. I bury my face in his chest in embarrassment and groan.

"What do you want for breakfast," I ask. I'd rather be in the kitchen cooking than enjoy his warmth. "You," he whispers. "What," I asked. His hands go back to my ass and he grabs tight.

I gasp and claw his chest. "I want your sweet lips around my cock. I want to taste that pussy of mine. I want to fucking fuck you from behind until you cum around my dick. Will you be able to give me all that for breakfast, babe," he said, nuzzling the side of my face.

I. Can't. Breath.

"You...need...You need to go," I finally said. His hands squeezed me for the last time then rested on his sides. "Yet you still on top of me Princess," he said with a smirk laced in his words.

Damn warm body. I slowly got off him and sat cross-legged on the other side of the bed. He chuckled. "That's a view I'd love to wake up to every morning, Princess," he said.

I looked at myself in confusion and... screamed. I screamed at seeing my own bare lady part. Oh. My. God. I rolled to the floor and yalped in pain.

"Are you okay, Princess," he said, gazing down on me from the bed. I scowl and pull my shirt lower to cover myself up. "Asshole," I mumbled. The look in his eyes darkened for a while.

"Be care of what comes out of that pretty mouth of yours, baby girl. I'd hate to make it impossible for that fine ass to sit," he said in a low tone. I swallowed. Hard. "Sorry," I mumbled.

"Good girl,"

chapter nine

~ Sir~

"You can't see her yet. I'll introduce you two when the time is right," I whisper yell at Duncan. I don't know what's going on in his dirty mind but he can't see Vivian...not yet. I'm blunt but I'm afraid that he'd scare her away from both of us. From me.

"Yes, I can and you will introduce me to her. As for the grip you got on me I suggest you let go of my collar before I bend you over and spank you with my belt," he growled. I gulped and quickly let go of him.

"Can I come with you then?" I ask, staring at the floor like It could open up and swallow him. I stare at the floor like it's the most fascinating thing in the world.

"Let's go baby boy," he said with a firm but soft voice. I clear my throat like that doesn't affect me. He chuckled and swatted my ass.

We entered the club and I spotted my Princess instantly. What she wore got two pairs of eyes darkening with anger. "What the fuck is she wearing?" Duncan asked. I shrugged and made my way to our private booth.

Duncan has shares in this club hence the reason why we had a private booth. He doesn't join me instantly though.

I stare at my baby girl dressed in black stockings with five inch stilettos. A leather dress that hugged her like second skin. She looked so fucking sexy and other man noticed it.

That made my fists clench. She's only doing her job. I told myself. My phone started ringing. "Yes?" I said as a greeting. No one said a thing. I scoffed and disconnected the call.

I checked the caller ID, it was David. Why was he calling me. I'll have to ask him when I get home. Everything is pissing me off tonight.

Duncan slid into the booth grinning like the cat that got the cream. "You're grinning," I said, eyeing him like he suddenly grew two heads. The grinning never stopped and his eyes were focused behind me.

What came next had me choking on my own saliva. "What did you do," I rasped between coughs. His flaming eyes continued staring at my Princess as she made her way towards us. "Fired her," he simply said.

Wait, what?

"You did what?" I yelled. The smirk on his face disappeared. With lightning speed, he was in my face choking...my dick. The grip on my dick was so painful.

" That's the second time you disrespected me tonight," he whispered. "I will not tolerate such behaviours in public." I bit my lip to stop myself from screaming In pain.

"Excuse me," a small voice said. Duncan glared at me for the last time before smirking. He got off me and sat beside me. "Yes little girl," he said.

Vivian stared at Duncan for a moment before looking at me. "Can I talk to you," she said. "Take a sit, little girl," Duncan said.

I could see that she was losing her patience and would likely receive a punishment. Instead of trying to get up, I watched my Princess dig her own grave. Some sadistic part of me was even excited.

"I'm sorry Mr but I'd like to speak to my boyfriend. Alone. And I'd really appreciate it if you stopped calling me little girl," she almost yelled.

The smirk on Duncan's face disappeared instantly. "I'd watch my mouth if I were you, baby girl," Duncan lowly growled.

"Sir, I want to talk to you alone… please," her voice broke at the end. I glare at Duncan and climb over him to my Princess. I sit on the other side of the booth and make her sit on my lap facing me.

As soon as her head made contact with my neck, she started shaking. I felt moisture on my neck and her small hands had a strong grip on my shirt.

I continued glaring at Duncan over my weeping Princess. He doesn't know it but this job kept her off the streets. His eyes had questions.

I shook my head, letting him know that it's not the right moment for his questions. " What's wrong, Princess," I asked even though I knew the answer.

Her tears came out harder as she silently cried on my neck. "She…sh…she f-f-fired me," she whispered. It was the first time I saw Duncan guilty.

He got up and came to our side of the booth. He pulled Vivian and made her sit on his lap. She buried her face into his chest and continued crying.

Well, I think we are going to be okay.

Chapter ten

~Duncan~

I've never been good at dealing with the shit I feel. Sometimes I come home angry and punish Sir. Make him cum so much until he couldn't anymore and then destroy me with my dick.

But right now I think I let my anger get the best of me. Guilt continues to eat me alive as I sooth the weeping girl on my lap. I really fucked up this time.

The disrespectful cutie next to me continues glaring at me and I ignore him. I'll give him my attention when I get home.

"I'm sorry," I whisper in her ear. She started taking deep breaths to calm down. My hand continues rubbing her back soothingly.

She slowly looks up at me and clear her throat. "Thank you," she whispers. I lean down and kiss her right then her left cheek before delivering one to her forehead.

"You can't kiss me in front of my boyfriend or kiss me in general. It's inappropriate," she firmly said trying to get off my lap. I tightened my hold on her.

"Sweetheart, I'm..." Sir kicked my leg. I glared at him. I'm sure he can manage cumming fifteen times tonight. That would make my weekend.

I smirk in his direction and he gulps before repeatedly clearing his throat .At least you know you gonna get it,boy.

~•~

~Sir~

Fuck my life. I can't believe I did that. It's going to be so damn hard to walk tomorrow. The fucker's smirk make me a little bit more scared of going home at the end of the night. Fuck.

The squirming girl on his lap reminds me of a very important revelation. I give Duncan the pleading eyes and lightly tug at Vivian. He kisses Vivian at the corner of her lip and let her go.

The frown on her face is priceless but there's no time to let her reaction to Duncan entertainment me. There are far pressing matters to attend to.

I settle my Princess on my lap and kiss her forehead. "Is he your friend? And why are you letting him touch me," she asked. I glanced at the smirking man beside us.

"Well, Princess...um this is Duncan." I swallow the lump that suddenly formed in my throat. I clear it. "And..."she said, folding her arms. The space between our upper body is not helping. At all.

Like a band aid,Sir. Like a fucking band aid, I told myself. "Duncan is...my boyfriend," I quickly said. I slowly opened my eyes to a wide eyed Vivian. Jaw on the floor and all.

"Okay," she whispered. Fuck. That's not a good sign."Princ-."Her head lowered and she sighed. "Can I go home now,"she asked in a small voice.

My grip on her tightened. "No. Let me..."She put her small hands over my lips. I licked her palm. She repeatedly shook her head.

"I have to process... everything. Specifically in the comfort of my home. I'll see you tomorrow," she said crawling on the table without looking at Duncan. Fuck.

I watched her small frame walk away and disappear facing my very pissed off Master. I gave him the puppy dog eyes with the cutest pout I can master. He chuckled.

"That's not going to get you out of this, pup ," he gruffly said. I sighed in exaggeration and his the excited smile on my face. "Ready to go?"

"Sure?"

chapter eleven

~ Vivian~

BeepBeepBeepI cover my ears with my pillow while searching for my annoying beeping alarm. I was so close to finally sleeping!So close! I internally yell.

Last night when I got back home without changing my clothes,I got into bed and thought I'd sleep. No such thing happened because my treacherous brain kept on repeating what Sir told me.

"Duncan is my boyfriend."

I still can't believe it. He, the hottest guy at college has a boyfriend. He's gay. That actually explains a lot. I never heard anything about Sir being in a relationship with any girl. Except me.

I rub my tired eyes and stretch my tired limbs. Time for job hunting, again. Ain't life sunshins and rainbows.

I get out of bed and drag myself to my tiny bathroom. Damn tiles are cold. I step into the shower and just let the water sooth me.Now it's time to go over last night's events.

I got fired for dropping a tumbler. That matter could have been resolved but Nikita refused to listen to me. I really liked working there plus they pay well. Moving on.

My boyfriend has a boyfriend. My boyfriend has a boyfriend. My boyfriend has a fucking boyfriend! I wonder why he was in a relationship with me. That's cheating. That makes me feel disgusted of myself.

I quickly finish showering and towel dried myself. I wrap a fluffy towel around me, not caring that it hardly covered my ass and made my way to the kitchen.

I made something for myself to eat. I heard a knock on my door and got up to answer it. The person I saw on the other side of the door wasn't expected. At all.

I stared open mouthed at him. He slowly made his way inside my home while I walked backwards. Thanks legs. He closed the door behind him and locked it."Hello, Vivian,"he said.

"Duncan?"

~•~

~Duncan~

"Duncan?"she whispered. Now I know why Sir chose her. There's something about her that calls out to the master in me. Cleared her throat.

"What are you doing here?" I roam my eyes around hr home. It's too small for a Princess like her. I finally settle my eyes on her.

Her cute glare makes me smirk . " I came to see you, sweetheart. What are you wearing?" I ask. She takes a look at herself and quickly turn around.

Now that's a view I would want to wake up to every morning. I thought while biting my fist. She takes a deep breath before facing me again.

"I like your determination sweetheart," I said folding my arms. " Okay,I do get the point that you and Sir have some kind of...a relationship and I apologize. I'm sorry that he cheated on you..."

That was my breaking point. Damn. It's been so long since I laughed like that. I clear my throat before making my way towards her and pin her against the wall. I lean into her neck and lightly bite it.

The moan that escaped her kissable lips made me want to dry hump her. What has this girl turned me? Fucking ten, again?

"You don't need to apologize, Kitten. I told him to look for a submissive for the both of us,"I said against her delicious skin. She shivered in response. So damn responsive.

"I...I... I'm not a... submissive," she whispered. I wrapped an arm around her waist and pulled her closer to me. She inhaled sharply. I grinned and licked the spot I bit her. She tasted as delicious as she smelled.

"You taste so good, Kitten," I said. "I'm going to let you go to your room,dress nicely. We going on a date,okay Kitten?" She nodded.

I kissed her on the forehead and gave her ass a tight swat. She screamed and sprinted to her room leaving me in tears from all the laughing.

I'm going to enjoy taming you, Kitten.

chapter twelve

~Vivian~

What the actual fuck happened. I ask myself as I pace the small space of my room. He commanded me and I just nodded like the Kitten i am.

Damn hate that pet name. Who are you trying to fool? The stupid voice in my head said. Damn voice.

I took a deep breath to calm my nerves. I really didn't understand what was happening to me but some sick part of me actually wanted it to happen.I wanted to go out with Duncan.

Be the subject of his beautiful menacing eyes. He really is gorgeous. I needed to stop pacing before I dug a hole on my floor.

I stomped my way to my tiny closet and quickly searched for something to wear. Nothing. I had nothing fancy enough.

Who are you trying to impress. The annoying voice in my head screamed. Shut the fuck up. I yelled back.

I'm losing my mind. I sat on the floor and stared at my clothes. Disappointed. It hit me then. I don't have fancy clothes or a job.

The first tear slowly tracked down my cheek. The the ones after it quickly followed.

I won't have enough money to pay for my rent next week. Or buy food. Or anything. I'll be a homeless orphan.

I head loud banging on my bedroom door. Did he hear me? I quickly wiped my tears as clean as I can and plastered a sequin smile. My steps to the door felt heavy.

I opened the door to a not expressed Duncan. " Why aren't you dressed yet?" He asked. I refused to open my mouth. I just stared at him.

" I asked you a question, Vivian," he arched a perfectly shaped brow. I couldn't stand the way he was looking at me.

Suddenly,he was slowly coming closer. His hand caressed my cheek. "Why are you crying baby girl?" He asked.

My own hand made its way to my cheek to investigate. The evidence was there,my cheeks were wet and getting wetter.

"Tell me what's wrong, Vivian," he said cupping both my wet cheeks. Before I knew what I was doing,my lips were on his.

And... I myself falling. I landed on the floor with a loud thud. I didn't have the energy to get up due to the pain I was feeling.

Duncan... Duncan pushed me. He actually pushed me. Why did he push me? I was so confused. I tried getting up but my head hurt too much to move it a lot.

Without saying a word...he left

Chapter thirteen

 Sir~

I was so anxious to see him. To see her. To see them together. God I'm so scared. Why did I agree on this dinner thing again?

Can you think when you are drunk on orgasms? The little voice in my hard asked. I rolled my eyes and continued staring at the front door.

I head his car park. Breathing became hard. The cold swear on my skin felt scorching hot.

I got up to investigate his arrival. He was... alone. Why is he alone? Where is Vivian? Fuck.

As soon as the front door opened I attacked him with questions. He just shook his head and went to the small bar and poured himself some whiskey.

"Answer me, Duncan. Where is she? What happened when you got there?" He downed the first glass in one go and poured himself a second glass.

"Stop drinking and answer my fucking questions, Duncan," I banged my fist on the table. He ignored me.

He took a deep breath and finally graced me with his beautiful eyes. I sensed danger from just that one look. "Come here," he simply said.

I slowly made my way to him but put a little distance between us. "Closer," he rasped. I did as I was told. Fuck. Why did I bang my fist on the table.

I'm so not going to enjoy what's coming my way. At all. His hand made its way to my throat. Not choking me though. I took a deep breath and looked him straight into his eyes.

"What happened," I whispered. Instead of answering me, his soft but firm lips touched mine in a gentle kiss. Okay...I didn't expect that.

The hand on my throat tightened with every soft kiss. I couldn't breathe anymore. I stopped kissing him back ass a sign of my suffocation.

He pulled back and stared at me. His menacing eyes told me everything I needed to know. He fucked up. Not just that. He fucked up bad. Really bad.

His hand loosened. I thanked God for the gift of air and continued staring at my boyfriend. "She was crying ,Sir. And I didn't know what to do. And then she kissed me and...I pushed her away," he said.

"Why was she crying," I rasped. He didn't answer me." Why was she crying, Duncan," I screamed. "Don't fucking talk to me like that," he screamed back.

I scanned the room for my keys. I need to fix this before we lost the best thing that has ever happened to us. He threw his keys at the bar table.

I took them and bid him good bye with a glare. The drive to Vivian's place felt longer than normal. My racing heart wouldn't allow me to calm down.

Her apartment door was wide open. When I entered, everything was still in place. I made my way to her room. She was on the ground. Silent tears tracking down to her ears.

I've never witnessed something as heartbreaking as that. I slowly made my way to her. She didn't open her eyes.

"Whoever you are, go ahead and rape me. While at it, kill me aswell. I got nothing to lose," she said. I felt my own tears tracking down my cheeks.

I got on my knees and picked her up. She didn't struggle. "Sir?" She asked. I didn't answer her. She borrowed her face into my chest and let the sobs wrack her body.

"I'm sorry Vivian. I should have never let him come here. I didn't know he was going to hurt you," I whispered. She shook her head. " It's not his fault," she rasped.

"I lost my job. By next week I'll be a homeless orphan and...and I don't have anything to wear to dinner," she exclaimed. Fucking Duncan.

"He didn't hurt you physically?" I asked. She shook her head. I took deep breaths and let her cry it all out. God knows how much she has been bottling up.

That job was really important to her. Duncan really fucked up this time. The next time he's drunk enough to let me be in control, I'm gonna make sure he doesn't sit down for a week.

I sat down with her on my lap. She felt calmer. More collected. When she tried getting up, I swatted her naked ass . She yalped.

"I'm sorry," she said. "I didn't believe it when people said that pretty boys came with baggage," she said. Inviting an awkward giggle in her tone.

I put both my hands on her hips and held on. She really was beautiful. Regardless of the puffy eyes and red nose. I chuckled.

"You can move in with me," I said. She froze. Fuck my big mouth. "I mean,you can live with me until you get another job," I corrected. Or tried.

Her big eyes were on me. "I can't do that,Sir," she sighed. "You have a fucking boyfriend. And I shouldn't be sitting on your lap or allowing you to comfort me. All this is inappropriate."

I took another deep break and borrowed my face into her neck. She smelled amazing. A contented sigh escaped her beautiful lips. A contradiction to what she just said.

That made me smile. Like the busturd that I am,I kissed her neck. I like that she's so damn responsive and soft. My sweet Vivian.

Chapter fourteen

~Vivian~

On a scale of one to a hundred, this situation is bordering on one thousand. I can't believe that I'm allowing him to touch me like this. Again.

More. The little voice in my head screams. My lady part clenches in agreement. Another moan escape my lips and I curse myself some more for loving every single minute of it.

He releases a deep groan against my skin. My toes curl painfully so. I tried pushing him away but that only made his hands to wader lower.

"I...want you...so bad," he rasped in the most chocolate dripping voice. I wanted to tell him take me already. Put me on my knees and do unspeakable things to my body.

But I couldn't. I had to remind myself that he's not just mine. He has a boyfriend. I know what Duncan said.

For a crazy moment I entertained the idea of being theirs. I've read enough books about those kind of relationships to not be surprised by them.

I felt a buzz against my naked butt. The vibration made me bite my lower lip to inhibit the traitorous moan from escaping my lips. I couldn't let him know how good he's making me feel.

Sir ignored his buzzing phone and continued showering my neck with kisses while his hands roamed my body.

"Sir...stop," I whispered. He ignored me too. If I allow this to continue, I'll end up doing something I'll regret . I cleared my throat and tried again. Louder this time.

He pulled back with a glow like groan and gazed at me. His list filled eyes were darker and more intense. Dangerously beautiful.

"Answer your phone," I said. His hold on me was still tight. He took out his phone and answered it without checking the caller ID.

"What?...No...Yes,master. No... I understand...She probably forgave you. ..Sure," I arched a brow. I'm guessing he's speaking to Duncan.

He put his phone against my ear. Silence. "You bored or something," I asked him. I heard him take a deep breath before he spoke.

"I'm...Uhm... Kitten." Stupid pet name. "I told you that my name is Vivian, not Kitten," I said. The look that Sir gave me was comical. I wanted to laugh but I reminded myself that I should be angry.

"I know. Vivian...I want to apologize for the way I reacted to you kissing me," he said, guilt laced in his tone.

My hands automatically went to my head like a reminder . Sir arched an annoyed brow and I just shrugged. "Okay," I said.

"What's that supposed to mean," he asked. I shrugged again then remembered that he can't see me. "Something?" I said. More like questioned.

I heard him take another deep breath. "Now listen. You are going to wear something comfortable and come to the house with Sir," he said. How stupid does this man think I am.

If sir could turn me into a moaning mess from just kissing and touching me, I wonder what he'll do. Much more dirtier things. The tiny voice in my head rejoiced.

I inwardly groaned at myself and sighed. "No," I simply said. "No?" He asked. "Yes...I mean No. I mean I won't be coming to your house." I said. Dammit.

"Oh Kitten." He chuckled softly. That sound warmed me to my toes. "Tell Sir to get kiss you good bye and get his sexy ass home. I need him since you won't be going out with us anymore," he said in a deeper tone than Sir's.

I'm sure Sir's pants have a cream spot on them from all the playing I have done. Too bad none of them will be getting rid of that arche deep inside me. I clenched my wall to make it more bearable.

Bad decision. That made everything worse. Sir grinned. Stupid beautiful face. It really should be illegal to be these beautiful.

"Your boyfriend said I must tell you to come home and never visit me ever again," I said, adding my own message into it. Sir raised an amused bro and chuckled softly.

I rolled my eyes which resulted in my ass receiving two spank . I yelped and covered my exposed ass. "I'll be home in ten minutes Master," Sir said without taking the phone away from my ear.

"Good. Enjoy your orgasm Kitten," Duncan said before disconnecting the call. My confused ass was slow to notice when Sir stood up.

He layed me down on my bed and roughly yank the towel from under me. The look in his eyes were of a predator praying on its next meal.

"What are you doing?" I asked. He got on the bed. Crawling his way towards me. For some weird reason I was excited. I wanted to be his prey.

"I'm doing as my master commanded me," he said. I licked my lips and waited for him to demonstrate the command.

He got between my legs and leaned closer to my face. I found myself leaning towards him too. The fuck are you doing? I asked myself.

When his lips made contact with mine my mind went blank. His wondering hand wondered from my neck to my lady part.

When his finger made contact with my clit,I jerked upwards. It has never felt that way when I touched it. It felt bigger... and hot.

He pressed on my little nubbin and made small circular movement. That had me literally screaming in pleasure.

He went faster and faster until I couldn't scream anymore. I found myself crying. Crying in pleasure? That a new one for me.

"Yes baby girl, that's it. That's it," he kept saying. "You going to come when I tell you to, okay," he continued. I nodded. Too occupied to say a word.

I felt a finger enter me. And that was it. I couldn't take this anymore. I've reached the top of the mountain and the only way to go was down.

"Please," I whispered. Too tired to scream it out anymore. "Let me cum. It hurts so bad," I contacted. His cruel smile told me everything I wanted to know. Beg.

So I begged until I couldn't hold it anymore. "Cum." He growled. And I came. Hard. Everything shook. He kept on driving his fingers in and out of me.

I think I just found heaven." You look so beautiful when you cum," he said. I girly giggle escaped me which caused me to clench some more around his fingers.

He took his fingers out of me and brought them to his lips. He licked them clean." Mmmm, delicious," he said. That made me want to beg him to fuck me. Good lord.

" When I call,you answer,we clear". I nodded. "Duncan is our master, yeah?" I hesitated before slowly nodding. " I don't expect you to be comfortable with this idea already but I'm hoping that you understand as soon as possible," he continued.

I just nodded. To everything he said. It might take me close to years to get used to having to boyfriends. I might even not get used to it. That's something I'll never admit out loud.

He got off the bed and went to my bathroom. I heard the shower turning on. He came back and gave me another searing kiss. "Go take a shower babe. I'll see you tomorrow."

And then he left.

chapter fifteen

~Vivian~

Job seeking really sucks big hairy donkey balls. I just got out of the fifth classy bar without an employment offer. They just take one look at me and dismiss me just like that.

I felt my ever silent phone buzz from my back pocket. I whipped it out and answered without checking the caller ID. "Sweet Vivian," Sir said.

Hearing his voice relaxed me instantly. I took a deep breath. " Ain't feeling sweet right now," I exasperated. He chuckled. "I can see that baby girl."

I saw him sitting on a bench three blocks from where I was standing. I waved at him. He waved back. I disconnected the call and made my way to him.

He instantly enveloped me in his arms. Damn he smelled so good. I breathed him in and sighed in content. It sure feels good to have a boyfriend.

"How about we grab some lunch and pay Master a visit. He sounded really stressed this morning," Sir said. My stomach appreciated the lunch part but not the visiting Duncan part.

I still can't come to terms with calling him my master. A girl really needs time to adjust to having two boyfriends. God.

I pulled back to look at him. His eyes were pleading with me to agree. I nodded. The smile he gave me transformed his face. He's so beautiful. I gave a hesitant smile of my own.

He stood up and led the way. We went to MacDonald's and ordered the share meal. Duncan's office was on a part of Snowville I've never seen before.

The drive there was shorter than expected. I wish it was longer so could prepare some more. I stared at Sir and gave him the cutest pout I could manage. He grinned and shoot his head.

At least I tried. He parked his car. He turned towards me with a raised bro. "Say it," he said. I continued staring at the building in front of us.

"Say what," I mumbled. His face inched closer to mine. "What are you doing?" I asked. He kept getting closer and closer until his lips were a hair's distance from mine.

" Kissing my girlfriend," he said before igniting my intestines. I gladly responded. His hands came up to my face to rest on my cheeks. What a nice way to ease my nerves.

What'd I say about boyfriends.

Chapter sixteen

~Duncan~

"Mr Mae called," Sophie, my secretary said. I ran my hards through my hair for the tenth time. Work this week has been brutally hard.

I swear I can't think straight. I took a deep breath and gave Sophie my attention. "Tell him to call back when he has come to a final decision," I tell her before swiveling my chair.

The view is really beautiful and calming. My head goes back to a moment I shared with Sir. He looked so beautiful pressed up against the floor to ceiling windows.

I take another deep breath. I wonder how Vivian will look on my desk though. A small smile played on my lips. A knock on my door disturbed my fantasy. Back to scowling I guess. I sighed.

Sophie poked her head again. "What is it now," I groaned. She cleared her throat. I turned around without opening my eyes. "You have visitors," she said in a soft voice.

"Tell them that I'm not available," I said turning back around. " Let's go,Sir," a sweet familiar voice whispered. My day just got even better.

I turned my chair to face the beautiful duo in front of my desk. "Well hello there," I rasped in my most seductive voice. Sir arched a brow. I chuckled.

"You too old for cheesy lines," he said, unimpressed. I arched my own brow. The floor suddenly became interecting to him. "What did I do that the gods gifted me with this visit today?"I asked.

Vivian continued staring at me which means that Sir dragged her along. He face looks so innocent. Too bad I know how she sounds when she cums.

That instantly made my pants tighten. I adjusted myself in my sit and sat at an angle. "We brought lunch," Sir said. Vivian walked forward with her hands behind her.

Fuck yes. I internally screamed. I licked my lips ready for some sweet pussy. She produced a paper bag from McDonald's.

"McDonald's?" I asked in an unusual tone. Sir was struggling with his laughter behind our girl. I glared daggers at him. He continued silently laughing.

"Don't you like it?" She asked. I stopped glaring at Sir and gave her my undivided attention. "What makes you say that," I asked. Wanting to listen to her sweet voice.

"I mean it's not my usual preference but it's okay," I reassured her. Her face lit up a little but no hint of a smile was evident. She nodded .

I made my way to the sitting area in my office. It consisted of couches covered by the softest silk material and a small coffee table. I sat down and motioned for them to come join me .

Sir was already close to the sitting area so it was just Vivian. She occupied the space between me and Sir. "Serve," I commanded. My eyes scanned her from her head to her gorgeous legs.

I found Sir watching me with the most lust consumed eyes. I licked my lips suggestively and his tounge stuck out like the good puppy he is. "Kneel," I mouthed.

Without standing, he got on his knees in front of Vivian. I also got on my knees. "What's going on?" she asked. Sir started kissing up her leg.

" Well...we have just decided that you'll be our lunch," I rasped. Her confused expression made me chuckle. I started kissing her other leg too.

"Open up, Kitten," I rasped. She hesitantly parted her legs. My lunch was wrapped up in black lacy panties. I bit the inside of her thigh and she gasped.

My hand darted out to grab Sir by the hair. The sexy whine-moan that escaped his lips made me even harder. I pulled his face towards mine and crashed our lips together.

This kiss was different more intense, or maybe it's because we have an audience. I heard the softest moans from above us. I stopped kissing Sir and focused on the moaning mess in front of me.

Sir had two fingers massaging her little nubbin through her underwear. I couldn't take my eyes off her. She looked so beautiful.

Now that's a true definition of a queen.

—

~Sir~

My baby girl moans away as I rub her little nubbin over her panties. Her soft moaning put Duncan in a trance. He's head keeps getting closer to her crotch. Probably inhaling the sweet scent of her juices oozing out of her.

I put more pressure on her clit eliciting louder moans from my baby. "Do you like what I'm doing to you," I asked in a hushed tone. She just moans in response.

"Words kitten," Duncan commands. That makes me look at him. His eyes lock with mine. He gives me a devilish grin. I smirk in return. "Yes M... master," Vivian groans in response.

The zipper on my pants suddenly becomes annoying. "Go lock the door," Duncan says. I do as I'm told and go lock the door. My dick sprung out when I unzipped my pants. I sigh in relief and get rid of the rest of my clothes.

Master tore the annoying material from Vivian's crotch. A partially annoyed whine escapes her cute lips. "I'll buy you more," Duncan said. I'm sure he would not appropriate me using his name in my head. That makes me chuckle.

Master quickly gets rid of her clothes and shower her beautiful body with kisses. I take a sit on the coffee table and observe Master with a woman.

"What do you want," he asked. Vivian whimpers from a kiss delivered to her left tit. I internally groaned. I want to have those glorious nipples in my mouth too.

Master latches on one and Vivian jacks forward in response. His other hand massages the other one. She tried closing her legs but master slapped them open again.

Getting in between them, he alternated between her beautiful breasts. My dick twitched and pre cum made its way up my tip. I used it as lube to rub myself.

"You got the most beautiful tits," Master said again her nipple. "I'm...I'm aching," she whispered back. That got me on my feet. "Where?" I asked kneeling behind master.

I grinded my hard member against his ass. The licking halted. He pushed his silk clad ass against my dick causing more Pre cum to come out.

I have never fucked master's ass. His mouth? Yes. Multiple times. But not his sculptured ass. I've fantasized about begging him to do it but never got the time. I'm always caught up in cumming and sucking cock.

I snake my hand around him and rub him over his boxer briefs. I peek over his shoulder and lock eyes with a dazed Vivian. I close my eyes and shower master's neck with kisses. I nip him then suck on the skin.

I could cum from just listening to him moan. I grind some more into him and fist him harder. "Sir," he moans. "Yes, Master's," I answer. "Kneel," he commands.

Vivian kneels infront of Master and comes closer. She starts kissing up his neck on the other side of his neck. I'm so proud of her.

I slide master's briefs lower and jacked him harder using his pre cum. A deep feminine groan caught me attention. I peeked over Master's shoulder again.

Master had two fingers inside our sweet pet. The fingers moved faster and faster eliciting loud moans. "You look so beautiful moaning for Master baby girl," I commented.

She continued moaning in pleasure, her head resting on master's other shoulder. "Yes she does," Master groaned. I sunk my teeth into master's shoulder and licked the spot.

"That's it," Vivian started chanting. Master increased his pace driving his fingers harder into her. We both watched in awesome as she climaxed around his fingers.

I went back to pleasuring Master as soon as her limp body fall to the floor. Unashamed of her spread legs shaking from satisfaction.

Thick ribbons of cum decorated her chest and pelvis. Master threw his head back and groaned as he came. I felt myself Cumming from just watching both my lovers cum.

I sucked on master's neck to hide my weakness. He chuckled knowing exactly what I'm trying to do. "Fuck me," he groaned." That was amazing," he commented.

I groaned in agreement. Vivian gave a weak smile. Master leaned towards and gave Vivian a searing kiss. "You were amazing," he said against her lips.

Master got up to go take a shower in his office bathroom. "Are you okay," I asked. She nodded too tired to utter a single word. I chuckled and pecked her forehead.

I picked her up and followed Master. After taking a shower, we ate the food from Macdonald's." How was job searching," Master asked.

" No one wants to hire me," she replied, shrugging like it's nothing. I ached my brows at Master in annoyance. She wouldn't be doing this if you just contained your jealousy.

He rolled his eyes at me and continued eating. "What do you want though. After college I mean," he asked without looking at her.

" I want to go into the publishing industry," she said. Master smiled. Already formulating something he'll regret. I have my own businesses due to that smile.

As much as I'm grateful for everything he has done for me, I'm not sure that she's going to like him very much. Imagine a 19 year old owning three strip clubs and two bars. All this has been overwhelming.

I'm so not ready for her reaction for what's coming her way

chapter seventeen

~Vivian~

Besides school and working at Mrs Halz, my life has been pretty shitty. Mr Williams has been leaving some wonderful news lately.

Turns out I have a week to settle my rent or I'll be homeless. Ain't that just awesome. I don't even know what to do.

What I know is that I won't be asking my concerned boyfriend for help. When he invites himself over, I make sure that I hide the letters in a place he won't find them. My darling tampon bag.

He's pretty snoopy but he has always avoided that bag. Right now I'm just laying on my floor going over my life. "What are you thinking about," my intrusive boyfriend asks.

At this point I gave up scolding him for doing that. "Nothing important," I reply. He aches an eyebrow at me. I roll my eyes at the ceiling.

"I saw that," he says. I raise my arm and give him a thumbs up . He chuckles and quickly yankl me to my feet. "Goddamnit." The giggles that escape my lips betray my annoyed facial expression.

When I open my eyes, I'm met by his beautiful eyes. "Hey baby," I say. He leans forward and kisses my forehead. "Hey baby girl," he says against my head.

I lean forward and inhale his delicious cologne. He smells so sexy I could just jump his bones. "Why are you sniffing me," he asks, amusement laced in his voice. "You smell so delicious," I say, sniffing him louder.

He chuckles and kiss my forehead again. "We need to talk about something," he says. That sentence makes me very nervous to be honest. Nothing good has ever came when someone said it.

"Okay," I said, creating space between us so I can see his face. "Let's sit down," he said directing me to my bed. I sat cross-legged and hugged my favourite pillow.

"What do you wanna talk about," I asked letting my nerves known. He cleared his throat and moved closer to me. I really am not going to like what he's about to tell me.

He cleared his throat again before he spoke." You deserve a punishment for keeping this from me and Master is not going to be any easy on you." Okay, I'm confused here.

" But I didn't misbehave. I didn't curse infront of you or Master. I haven't caressed myself since you told me not to do it in your absence. So I'm confused here," I say raising my voice a little.

He raises an unimpressed bro and frown. I probably should have not done that. My point is I've been as good as I can be lately. I don't deserve any punishment. Damnit.

"Why didn't you tell me that you are about to be evicted," he says in an unusual calm tone. The kind of tone Master uses when he's not liking something. Fuck.

Shoot. How did he know about that. I thought he hasn't snooped in my tampon bag . That was a dumb thought I guess.

"It's nothing important," I say getting off the bed. I'm pulled back by my wrist. "Nothing important," he says. I can feel his anger through the tight hold of my wrist.

"Sir," I warn, staring at my poor wrist. It's not like I'm not used to it but I'm not liking it very much right now. My gaze moves to his face.

"Why are you even mad," I exasperate. " It's not like you are the one going to be homeless!" I yell. In a blink of an eye I'm on my back, hands trapped above me.

His face is so close I could kiss him." Who the fuck are you talking to like that," he growls against my ear. A shiver runs down my spine. I close my eyes in excitement.

"I am mad cause you won't be having a roof over your head," he says in a deep tone. "And I gave you a chance to tell me...but you chose not to. Why?," he continues.

"Because you'll tell Master and he'll do exactly what you are doing," I yell. I expected him to tell me to watch my tone or yell back but he doesn't.

He let's go of my hands and gets off me. He settles on the edge of my bed. He sighs and runs his fingers through his hair.

I remain the way he was holding me. "I'm sorry," I whisper. "Lidia said she'll give me a raise so I can be able to pay for my rent," I lie.

Lidia Halz is the most insensitive women I have ever met. She even scolded me and threatened to fire me for "begging" her. God knows I wasn't. I even offered to work extra hours for the raise.

Sir won't be made privy to that information. He might just drag me to Master and punish me. Well...what doesn't kill him makes him stronger,right.

I'll probably be the one dying. "Vivian," he rasped. I hope he isn't mad anymore. "I'll only tell you this once and I won't take no for an answer." Okay...I really am not going to like this.

" You'll be moving in with me and Master tomorrow,"he said, preparing to leave by the looks of it."Wait,what?" I screeched. God please make what he said a mistake.

" I expect you to be done packing by tomorrow morning and ready to go,"he said nearing my bedroom door. "No!" I yelled. "If you won't do it, I'll come get you myself. Ready or not," he said ignoring me.

"No!" I chanted until I couldn't hear the light falls of his foot steps. The front door was banged closed. I slumped back on my bed in shock.

What have I gotten myself into!

Chapter eighteen

~Sir~

"You did what," Master whisper yelled. When I got home last night the house was dark and quiet. I didn't have the chance to recap everything to him.

" She's moving in with us today," I repeat using much more simpler words. He throws the covers off his body and stalk to the bathroom naked.

I thought he'd like having his pet closer so he can play with her. To be honest I didn't expect this kind of reaction. To say I'm disappointed will be an understatement.

I hear water running in the bathroom and decide to go ahead and make breakfast. Maybe he'll change his mind after a cup of coffee.

I made coffee for myself cause God knows everyone needs it. Half way through making breakfast I hear foot steps coming downstairs.

"Hey babe," I greet like we didn't just wake up on the same bed. He rolls his eyes at me and snatch some strawberries from my plate.

The sizzling of meat in oil captures my attention. "Don't come near me. I burn your lovely skin," I say giving the food my attention again.

A hard member is pressed against my back. I bite my lip to prevent the wanton moan from escaping my lips." Your body is betraying you my sweet puppy," he groaned in my ear.

I grinded my ass into him eliciting a soft groan out of him. "Wouldn't it be great to have your sweet Kitten here as well," I asked innocently.

He borrowed his face into my neck. Wet,hot open mouthed kisses made me moan a little. His wondering but determined hand made its way into my sweats.

The light grip on my dick did magical things to my body. "I'm cooking,Master," I moaned. He just ignored me and continued jacking me.

"You want me to stop," he whispered into my hear. I shook my head. I would be a crazy man if I told him to stop. I quickly turned off the stove and leaned into him.

I couldn't hold back my moans anymore. I let him have it all. My groans and moans. After all,they belonged to him.

I belong to him

———————————————

~Vivian~

I paced the small expanse of my bedroom as I waited for Sir. I tried calling him last night. None of my calls went through.

I don't think he understands that this is a serious matter. The only option I'm left with is calling Master, which I'm so not doing. I'm sure he's the one who suggested this asinine idea.

It's times like this I wished I had friends. On top of being an orphan, I went and choose to keep to myself. Damnit.

"Answer your fucking phone, Sir," I mumble under my breath. Straight to voicemail. Again. I throw my phone to my bed and plopped my ass on my floor.

What have you gotten yourself into. The annoying tiny voice in my head whispers. I mentally tsk myself and rest my head on my knees.

Movement at my front door has me jumping to attention. I don't know where he got my spare keys. Damn intrusive boyfriend.

Before the door is fully open, my lips are ready to give reasons. They die in my throat as soon as Master makes eye contact with me.

How can a person be so godly beautiful. The small voice in my head chimed. "Hello Kitten," he muttered. A small smile marked my face.

The words refused to come out. I gave him a tiny wave and did a full one eighty to my room. I head him chuckled.

I swear it doesn't matter that this man has seen me naked. When I see him, my nerves get all over the place. And my traitorous body makes it obvious. Damnit.

"You ready to go," he inquired. I sat on my comfortable bed. I stared at the spot beside his head. Looking at him won't do me any good.

I cleared my throat a few times. "Master, about that," I started. God you sound pathetic. The little voice in my head piped. Goodness. Do I hate myself or something?

"I'm listening," he said, aching a perfectly shaped brow. I took a few deep breaths and looked him square in the eye. " I don't want to move in," I stated.

Ha made his way to my bed and sat besides me. His warm hard caressed the small of my back. That single touch sent shivers down my spine.

I tensed my body to hide my reaction to him touch. Failed. He grinned at my traitorous body. I rolled my eyes and tried not to focus on the hand currently making me feel stuff.

"That decision isn't yours to make any more Kitten," he stated. Crumbling my last wall of hope to the floor. I gazed at the non existent debris in sadness.

"But you can't do that to me." My voice broke. Was I seriously about to cry. No. That can't happen infront of him. Again. I'm sure he already thinks that I'm a cry baby who can't handle her problems.

His features softened a little. "Don't cry Kitten," he said while rubbing my back. I furiously wiped at the few tears that wouldn't listen to me.

"Okay, tell you what. Just move in with us for a month and if you don't like it, I'll get you your own apartment," he said. I let my brain process that for a while.

Not paying so many bill sounds like music to my ears. I'll pay him for my stay at his house with whatever little I have.

I'll be graduating college next month meaning I can finally get a stable job. I nodded in agreement." I let it slide before but not anymore Kitten. You can talk so use your words," he growled.

I stared at him like he's crazy. Damn man with hot tampers . I rolled my eyes at him just to get under his skin. His jaw tightened.

I smiled and battered my lashes innocencly. "Okay," I replied. His tightened features relaxed.

The rest of the day was a blur of loading everything I owned into a truck. We made our way to their home in his fancy car.

Here we go again

Chapter nineteen

~Vivian~

On our way to his house, we stopped at MacDonald's and got some food. I ate while Master replied to some emails.

I spent the rest of the journey asleep. I only woke up when I felt myself being lifted off the car sit. "We there yet," I asked in a small tired voice.

"Yes Kitten. Go back to sleep." He ordered. That's one order I'll obey willingly everytime. I layed my head on his chest and dozed off. Comfy.

My body made contact with a soft mattress. A warm body pulled me towards it. I cuddles into it with a contented smile on my face.

"Good night baby girl," Sir whispered against my ear. I mumbled something along those lines and cuddled deeper into him. Another body hugged me from behind sandwitching me.

~•~

Morning came and there were no man on either side of my body. The most delicious scent filtered into the room.

I threw the sheets off me and made my way to the bathroom. Urinated and brushed my teeth. After looking somehow presentable, I begun searching for the kitchen.

This house is pretty huge...and beautiful. I wonder why I missed the chance to tour it yesterday. Duncan ran so many errands I ended up sleeping in his car.

I gave up searching and just wondered around. Taking my own sweet time at it too. Though my stomach reminded me every once in a while that I haven't fed it yet.

Muffled moans reach my ears from the room I'm currently admiring. My curious mind had my feet tip toeing to the source. The moans were mixed with sweet manly groans.

I peeked through an opening through the door. What I saw had my jaw on the floor. Master had Sir bent over the kitchen counter. What he was doing to him had my panties wet.

"Master," he moaned. Duncan pressed something on his phone. "Yes Puppy," Duncan groaned. I watched in absolute silence. Admiring my boyfriends in their gorgeous nakedness.

Only a fool would dare to disturb such a show. Apparently, that fool is me. My dumb ass lost its balance and fall. The groaning and moaning in the room halted.

Fucking clumsy ass. Why did I have to lean on the damn door. Wasn't the small opening enough? I groaned in pain and... embarrassment.

Mostly embarrassment. Damn. I just watched other people have sex. I mentally face palm. Very nice Vee, real nice. Creep.

"I was looking for the kitchen," I lamely uttered. Master chuckled. His hips put me in a trance as they slowly moved.

"Fuck," Sir moaned. Fuck indeed. The little voice in my head agreed. I really need to get rid of that. As if.

"Come here," master ordered. It's not like we haven't been in this situation before. Although it was mostly him or Sir fucking me while they kissed or jacked each other off...Or sucked on each other.

" I didn't mean to disturb you," I mumbled, attempting to right myself. "I know Kitten. Now get your beautiful ass over here," he repeated. I gulped.

I slowly made my way to him. Sir was biting his lower lip so hard. I'm sure he doesn't want me to hear him sounding like a 'cock slut' like he always says I do.

When I got closer to Master, his hand shot out and grabbed me by the throat. Not too hard though. Just enough to have my heart racing in anticipation.

"Mmmm," he groaned against my neck. "You smell so good in the morning," he added. My hungry eyes went straight to where they were connected.

"Like what you see," Master asked. I nodded and licked my lips. I've only ever witnessed this on my laptop. They have never fucked in my presence. I swear my eyes were glued on them.

" Master, I think our little girl wants to play," Sir rasped. I did want to play but the how part was a mistery . Those X rated movies I used to watch always left me shook.

How the fuck are those girls able to take two guys at once? It was both empowering and terrifying at the same time. Of cause it didn't get past my fantasy list. Until now.

Master kept his lazy eyes on my face. I refuse to let him see how turned on I was. I refuse. He hummed in delight and smirked. He pulled out of Sir and looked at me.

" On your knees," he commanded. My list filled orbs gazed up at his list filled orbs. He had the most beautiful and mesmerizing eyes. Oh Lord, have mercy on me. That must be a serious criminal offence.

"Don't make me repeat myself," he hissed. I bent my knees until they made contact with the floor. He hummed in approval. I swear my stomach did a little dance.

Warm hands trailed the sides of my rib cages. Sir. His soft lips scorched my neck with open mouthed kisses. "Morning baby girl," he whispered against my ear. I just kneeled there, sighing in content.

"I need to get to work but firstly, I need to give you something to remember the whole day," Master said, stroking the hard member between his legs.

"Sir, come here," he commanded. Sir crawled from behind me to kneel in front of Master. Master grabbed Sir by the head and pushed him towards his dick. Sir gladly opened his mouth and welcomed Master. He groaned in pleasure.

I couldn't help but clench my pussy walls. Master's groans made my body tingle in the most unthinkable way. A thought crossed my mind and I too crawled towards Master. His half closed eyes followed my every movement.

I leaned closer and started kissing from his hip to his thigh, careful not to disrupt Sir. I got under Sir and started sucking on his balls.

"Jesus, women," Master moaned. I smiled around his ball. Sir quickened his movement a little. I felt Master shaking from being stimulated by us.

"Fuck. Stop that or I'll blast down your throat," he growled. Like the obedient girl I am, I stopped. A hard slap was delivered on my ass.

Sir's eyes were on me. I swear he was commanding me not to stop. So I leaned forward again and continued sucking.

With a loud growl, Master emptied himself inside Sir's mouth. Slowly fucking his face in the process. "God," he whispered. Sir released Master's dick with a pop and that was my cue to stop.

"Fuck, I wanted to ruin your pussy so bad," he commented. I smiled in victory.

Too bad you can't.

Chapter Twenty

~Sir~

When Duncan finally left for work, Vivian and I ate our breakfast in silence. I know that she did not want to come live with us.

I also understand her reasons but I can't have my baby roaming around, homeless. That wouldn't be me. I have experience with that and she is not ready for that kind of trauma.

"You going to class today," I asked. She just nodded. My brows furrowed. She was literally smiling and all when Duncan was here. Women.

She finished her food and washed her and Duncan's plates. My eyes followed her every movement. Her silence started to grate on my nerves.

When she passed me, I shot my hand out and grabbed her by the throat. I didn't actually choke her, just held her in place.

"Why are you not talking to me," I grumbled. Her silence towards me is seriously unnecessary. I want it to stop. Now.

"I need to get ready for class," she mumbled. Not looking at me. What the actual fuck is going on. "Not too long ago you were okay. What happened now?" I asked.

She gave me a bored look attempted to slap my hand away. I caught that hand too and held it above her head. "What is wrong with you?" I asked again.

Her defiant eyes held their ground. I want to discipline her so much right now, but I know she's mad. She just needs to stop behaving like a brat and tell me so I can apologize.

"Let me go," she whisper yelled. Fuck. This girl is seriously testing me. "Tell me what your problem is and I'll let you go," I growled.

She glared at me. This fucking girl...I swear. " You sent Master to come get me," she yelled in my face. The grip on her neck quickly tightened.

Her eyes widened in realisation before the went back to their defiant gaze. My nose flaired in annoyance. The fuck does she think she's talking to like that?

I took a deep breath to calm down before I did something I'll regret. Her neck was already bruised from my tight grip. That should have me at her feet, asking for forgiveness but I'm too mad to be caring.

"To begin with, I did not send Master to come get you. He just left without telling me anything–" I whispered against her ear." –And secondly, don't forget who the fuck you talking to," I added.

She nodded. "Words," I commanded. I swear she forgets that I'm still her daddy. Matter of fact, I have never heard her call me that.

"Who am I," I asked. Grinding my pelvis again hers. Her eyes fluttered close. That's right. Feel me. Her lips parted slightly.

"Who the fuck am I," I growled. Soft moans left her beautiful lips. "Sir," she whispered. I grinded harder again her making sure her clothes brushed her tiny nubbin.

"Wrong," I growled. I let go of her arm and cupped her warm pussy. So warm. I internally moaned. I rubbed her against her panties.

"Daddy," she whispered. I rubbed her faster. " Louder," I groaned. It didn't matter what Master had fucked me to last the whole day. I still wanted to 'ruine her pussy'. That thought had me smiling.

"Daddy...goodness that feels so good. So fucking good" she screamed. I pushed her panties aside and shoved two fingers into her molten heat. Her walls instantly clamped down on my fingers.

"That's right,I'm your daddy. And daddy doesn't promote disobedience baby girl," I groaned. Speeding up my movements.

Her sweet moans were music to my ears. I didn't want her to stop until she came around my fingers. Too bad her disobedience is going to be both our punishment.

"Yes,yes, yes. Oh my...that's it. That's it... please don't stop," she screamed in my face. That ,I allow. My sweet girl. I thought.

When I felt her stomach muscles tighten, I stopped. Moved her panties back in place and sucked on my fingers. I moaned in delight. Delicious.

I left her gasping form leaning against the wall. When I turned the corner,I heard a loud scream. I chuckled . Serves you right, Kitten. I thought.

I went straight to our shared bedroom and took a second shower. My throbbing dick resented me. I don't have time to touch myself so a cold shower will do.

I heard another door slam and I heard water running. I found myself grinning. Totally worth a throbbing dick. I thought.

When I was ready, Vivian was no where in the house. She must have already went to college. I took my car keys and made my way to college too.

I'm so going to enjoy my day.

~•~

~Vivian~

When I finally got to school,my nerves were all over the place. I was frustrated. Mad frustrated and I wanted revenge.

Hence the reason why I chose this outfit today. It is too revealing for my liking. Fuck,I look like one of the girls in college. Slutty.

My outfit consisted of a black cosette that ascenurated my cliverge with a very short skirt that reached the middle of my thighs. I paired it with black and white Vance.

I took a few deep breaths before exiting my car. The annoying cat calls that followed me made my skin crawl. The confidence I had when I chose this outfit was no where to be found.

Fuck. I need to get out of here.

When I turned the corner,an angry mouse with its followers was glariy at me. I gave her a blank look." What do you want," I asked. She just looked me up and down before scowling.

It's not like I'm dressed sluttier than her. The fucking tramp. "Imitating me,I see," she said. I wanted to laugh so goddamn much.

"Me? Imitate you?-" I chuckled. "-Get over yourself babes," I added. I internally cringed at myself. She really was the inspiration behind this.

"I need to get to class," I said, side stepping her. She grabbed me by the wrist. Digging her evil claws into my skin. "Let go of my wrist," I threatened.

I felt her nails pierce my skin and a little blood came out. "I said let go of my fucking wrist," I said through clenched teeth. She smirked before letting go of my wrist.

"Watch yourself, slut," she threatened before bumping her shoulder against mine. Whore. I thought. I rushed to the bathroom before going to class.

By the time lunch time came, I was already sick of my day. This clothes really made my day horrible and the person I was trying to punish wasn't even here.

More annoying cat calls were thrown my way when I made my way to the cafeteria. I got my food and sat down at my usual table. In the corner, far away from everyone.

I took out a book to read while I was eating. A door slammed against the wall. The usually loud room suddenly became quite. You could literally hear a paper clip falling.

Like always, I ignored them and continued reading. I appreciate the silence anyways. A shadow fall over me. By the looks of it, it was a boy.

"I dare you to fucking touch me this time Samuel. I'll break your fucking fingers. Mistake or not," I whisper yelled. The person behind me didn't move. Fucking annoying boys.

"I said get the fuck away from–" I was pulled by the hair. My eyes screwed closed and a string of curses left my lips.

When I opened my eyes, I smiled. If looks could kill, I'd probably be dead by now. I wanted to giggle so damn much but the grip on my hair was boardering to painful.

"Get up," he whispered. I shook my head back and forth. That made him angrier. The smile on my face began to hurt.

He let go of my hair and packed my stuff. Without even warning me, he yanked me out of my sit. All eyes were on us which did not sit well with me.

I couldn't stop smiling. He did not stop until we were in the girls bathroom. He threw me in side and slammed it behind him. "On your knees," he growled.

I gave him a bored look and folded my arms. I'm not kneeling on this dirty floor. He slowly walked towards me. It was only logical that I walked backwards.

"You dare disobey me," he asked. I looked at the floor. It was clean but I didn't know how clean it was. "The floor is dirty," I uttered.

"Is it?–" He retorted. "–You didn't think it was dirty when you practically dressed like a dirty slut," he added. That made me smile a little.

"Oh, you think this is funny huh?" He asked I shook my head back and forth. My back hit the cold tiled walls of the bathroom.

He smirked. "Okay then. Since you choose to dress like a dirty slut, I'll treat you like a fucking dirty slut," he rasped before taking hold of my shoulders.

He quickly turned me around. Shoving my upper half into the wall. I spread my palms against the wall to prevent an unwanted fall.

"Finally," I whispered. The smirk on my face really hurt. My lady parts are practically singing in joy right now.

His movements halted. I heard him laugh. "You cunning, fucking slut," he whispered, suprise laced in his voice. Wait, what's going on?

"I understand now. You did all this cause I left you hanging in the morning," he uttered. Fuck. I pushed my ass against his front, shame forgotten.

I didn't expect him to catch on this quick. I was so goddamn close. Damn. I leaned my head against the cold wall. I turned around and glared at him.

I straightened my clothes and side stepped him. Now it was my turn to get angry. Sir was laughing so hard that it really felt like spikes against my ears.

When I opened the door, Tyson and Liam fall on the floor. I snarled at them. The quickly got up and flashed me suggestive looks.

I rolled my eyes at them before making my way to the parking lot. I swear someone would have thought that I was being chased.

Running in heels is really hard and uncomfortable. The only thought in my mind was to go home and sleep my day away. I'm already sick of it.

My daddy is going to pay for this.

chapter twenty two

Vivian

I can't breathe. I can't fucking breath and I don't know what's stopping me from doing so. My eyes shoot open and I attempt to move.

That proves to be an impossible task. There are way too many limbs on top of me. God. I still can't fucking break.

I wiggle violently to rouse the monsters I'm sandwiched between. They groan in their sleep. Damn. How small am I people.

"He...jackasses... Can't breath," I manage to wheez out. They continue slumbering like i have all the air in the world. Damnit.

A crazy idea crosses my oxygen deprived mind. I turn my head and sink my teeth into Master's flesh as hard as I can. Damn muscles are painful.

"Fuck," he yell, yanking his arm away from my teeth. That actually hurt. " Can't breath," I wheez again. His eyes widen and he frantically remove his and Sir's limbs from my body.

I take a much appreciated deep breath and glare at him. "Are you okay Kitten," he asks. I nod . "Shit. How long have you been up," he asks.

" Not too long," I whisper. My eyes move to his bleeding arm and I start to panic. Fuck. Fuck. Fuck. I hurt him. I quickly get up and fuss over him.

"I'm sorry," I rush to apologize. He just stared at me like I'm crazy. I hurt this idiot and he's looking at me like I grew a second head. Man.

"It's nothing. Stop fussing Kitten," he rasped. I roll my eyes and quickly head to their bathroom. It takes me a while to find the first aid kit and head back to bed.

I clean up the wound and bandage it. I smile when it doesn't move. "Happy?" Duncan asks. I nod and pepper the bandaged area with soft kisses.

He chuckles and kiss my forehead. I giggle and the sleeping hunk choose that particular moment to wake up. "What's going on," he asks in a sleepy, gravelly tone.

I smile and give his head a kiss. "Good morning, Daddy," I say sweetly. I'm sure he's going to make me pay for scaring him the way I did last night.

Serves him right. I giggle and pet his head. I giggle some more when he slaps my hand away from his head. " You awfully in a good mood today," he says, annoyance laced in his words.

I put some more sugar into my smile and bat my lashes at him. When his eyes narrow into slits, a full blown laugh escapes me.

God. I'm really going to be punished for this. Master just watches us in silence, grinning at Sir. "Where were you last night," Sir asks. Like Master, I grin at him.

"Don't make me repeat myself Vivian," he says in a threatening tone. I continue staring at my Daddy. The anger on his face unfolds in wave. I look at Master's amused face and giggle.

Since he's not saying anything and finding this whole thing amusing, I continued my silence. Suddenly there's a hand in my hair. Tugging my head back ever so gently.

I whimper and try to look at Master." He asked you something,Kitten," Master whispered against my ear.

I swallowed the bratty words that would probably get me in more trouble and opted for a whimper. He tugged on my hair even more.

I attempted to give him a sweet smile but I'm sure I looked like a little devil with my eyes wide open and my smile all toothy.

He chuckled and loosen the grip on my poor hair. I whimpered in relief. "I see you aim on being a brat this morning," he mused.

I shook my head. "Master," Sir called, gaining both our attention. Even though looking at him strained my eyes. Master kept my hair in his fist.

"Yes pup," he replied. Pup. A small giggle escaped my lips. Now the spotlight was back on me. I mentally cursed myself. Dumbass.

"What is amusing that it made my Kitten giggle," Master asked. I blinked at him like I didn't hear him. I'm not saying shit. My mouth only gets me in trouble.

I'm aware that that might get me in more trouble but atleast it's gonna be a mild punishment. Master took a deep breath. Probably annoyed with my silence by now.

My conscious screamed at me to say something now. Well,me and her aren't exactly friends so I ignored it.

Goodness...

Chapter Twenty one

~Duncan~

When I got home from work, the house was quite. Usually my two lovers would be watching TV or something. Not tonight though.

All the lights were off. "Sir," I called. They probably went to get food. I took out my phone and speed dialled him. He answered on the second ring.

"Master," he said breathless. "Where the hell are you," I asked. If he's doing what I think he's doing, I'm going to rip him a new asshole. Literally.

"Has Vivian returned home," he asked. And that's when I remember that I haven't checked her room or the time. It was 2am. I quickly made my way to her room.

I switched the lights on. She stired and went back to sleep. Fuck. I exhaled in relief. God, this fucking women.

I slowly dragged my tired form to her bed. Little by little, the fabrics on my body were no more. I pulled back the covers and slid in.

She instantly cuddled me before I even got comfortable. Her body was so soft. So warm. So cuddleable. I took a deep breath.

This is nice. Very nice. But something is missing. I turned my head towards the night stand. A picture of me and Sir stood proud next to her phone.

That had me smiling like a pussy whipped idiot. It hasn't been that long but the thought of losing the angel nestled against me had me pissed.

I put both my arms around her. She inhaled in content. I reached for her phone. Sir's number was on speed dial.

He answered on the first ring. "Baby girl, I'm so sorry. So,so, sorry babe. I promise not to tease you like that ever again. Please come back home," he said. I wanted to laugh so damn much but the emotion in his voice sobered me.

"Come back home babe. She's safe," I rasped. He took a few deep breaths before telling me that he was on his way.

After a few minutes I head the front door slam closed. I'm spent and the beautiful cuddled beside me makes it very hard to keep my tired eyes open.

"Master," Sir calls. I try to speak but I'm too tired to utter a word so I just lay there and wait for him to find us. I heard hard foot falls coming this way.

The door opens and my gorgeous puppy graces the room. He looks as spent as I do. I give him a tired smile and he returns it.

He makes quick work of his clothes and slides on the other side of the sleeping beauty. He leans forward and pepper Vivian with open mouthed kisses along her neck to her jaw.

I watch silently. Content with my life. I raise my head slightly and welcome the waiting lips of my lover. I end the kiss before it heats me enough to want to make it hard for him to walk in the morning.

I kiss his cheek, a silent good night. He sighs in content and cuddle close. I finally allow my eyes to close.

I could get used to this

chapter twenty three

~Sir~

I watched her silently as she dug her own grave even more while Master's patience slowly fades. Leaving that punishment happy monster I grew to love.

He took another deep breath. I'm actually excited about this. She deserves to be thoroughly punished for scaring me the way she did last night.

She hasn't even told me where she went last night. I'll make sure to serve my punishment when Master's not around. I could hear myself crackling like a villain in the back of my head.

She surely was not home because I looked everywhere. Even in the basement I'm terrified of . Paranormal shows ruined them for me.

Master chuckled lowly, already planning on how to punish the little brat between us. I mentally smiled. Don't want him to notice my giddiness, do we.

"Pup, get me that new toy I got for our little princess," Master commanded with a smirk. Like the good puppy I am, I quickly went to the closet.

There was a hidden section where he kept all his favourite punishment tools. Though I stopped giving him reasons to punish me with them anymore.

Except for the casual disobedience tantrums I throw. The sex is much more intense when there's pain laced in it. Does that make me a pain whore? Yes. Yes it does and I love it.

I fidled around the many butt plug, vibrators and other objects and retrieved the leg spreader.

When Master bought it,I thought he was exaggerating since Vivian spread her legs just fine. She's a good cock whore like that.

I chuckled in excitement as I made my way back to our bedroom. The bed was bare of it's charcoal sheets and the pretty brat was already tied to the bed.

I gave her an evil smirk, already enjoying the show before it begun. "What," she sassed. I chuckle escaped my lips before I could stop it.

"Out of everything you could do this morning,you chose to piss Master off," I said, showing her the tool in my hands.

She rolled her eyes at me. I swallowed the urge to throw myself at the bed and fucking the brat out of her. I'm still your dominant, Vivian.When he's done,it would be my turn. I mused in my head.

"You gonna pay for that," I said, moving closer to the well adorned bed. She closed her legs cutting my view of her pussy off.

You won't be doing that anymore, sweetheart.

Master chose that exact moment to grace us with his presence."Has she begun to explaining her whereabouts?"he asked. I shook my head.

He smirked at the pretty brat we call our girlfriend. She began tugging violently at the restraints on her hands. That made me grin like the devil.

"Have you showed her my newest equipment," Master asked without looking at me. His attention was solely on his Kitten.

"Yes, Master," I said, handing the leg spreader to him. He let out a low satisfied groan while looking at the leg spreader.

"Take a look at this Kitten because it's going to be your undoing. By the time I'm done testing this bad boy, you will be bagging me to stop," he said while admiring the leg spreader.

She snotted. "Yeah, well there won't be any begging from me, Mr," she retorted emphasing the last word. Master ached a daring brow.

I stared back at him. He sighed dramatically and shook his head." I'm sick of your bratty attitude. Time to correct it," he said while spreading her legs and attached the leg spreader.

I would be lying if I said the little brat's calm facade continued cause it didn't. As soon as she was spread eagle, her breathing became more erratic.

Master gave her an evil smirk which meant he noticed. She closed her eyes and took deep breaths to calm down. I sat back on the bed and prepared myself for the show.

"Ready, Kitten," Master whispered.

_____Hey lovelies Hope y'all are doing fine. I've finally decided that this chap has been in my drafts for too long and I want y'all to have it. I know it's shot but remember that I love every one of you

-bunny

Chapter twenty four

~Vivian~

The thought of being punished had my breathing erratic. I'm sure Master thought I'm scared but it was actually the opposite.

The anticipation did all this to me. Sir on the other hand looked very excited. Also assuming that I'm scared I presume.

"Eyes on me , kitten," Master growled. I obeyed his command and looked at him. I swear he gains layers of beauty every day. He's hella fine I tell y'all .

"I should be spanking your ass red but I think you've become immune to that ," he rasped and he began crawling towards the headboard. This made me feel like a prey.

"Master," Sir called. We both looked at him." Yes, puppy," Master replied smirking like the predator he was. That made me shiver.

" I know what you could use," he said. My eyes widened. Master does not hide his punishment happy personality which does not scare me.

Sir on the other hand was a covert punishment happy monster. Master may not know this due to being his Dom. My wide eyes narrowed to slits.

The fucker had the nerve to steal a glance at my naked form. Master nodded for him to proceed. Sir quickly got off the bed and rushed to the closet.

"Isn't he the cutest?" Master asked. I blinked up at him. The cutest? On normal circumstances I would agree with him and add some more compliments but not now. Right now I think he's anything but cute.

I scowled at the insane fucker beside me. He chuckled and trailed his hand along my leg. His touch felt hot. Very hot.

We head shuffling and Sir emerged from the closet holding a cloth that looks to be hiding something. I stared at it as it got closer and closer to the bed.

He layed it down on the floor and grinned at me. My scowl deepened if that's even possible. Master chuckled some more.

" What do you have there,Pup," Master asked. Sir looked at him with the most innocent eyes and demon can master. Yes. That's exactly what I saw at that moment. A demon.

"It's nothing serious Master. Just a few toys I bought not too long ago," he said. I tried to create some distance between me and Master.

"Is that so,Pup," Master asked. Sir nodded. "Okay then, let's get started shall we," Master said.

I take back my words. I'm not excited. I'm terrified for my life. If I was not tied to this bed,I would have ran as fast as I could.

Master reached out his hand and Sir gave him something. It looked like a string...with balls. Huh? What was he gonna do with that?

"You look confused," he said, studying the string. I am confused. Not even the many books I read would prepare me for this.

"Where is that going?" I asked. The demon on the floor looked ready to give an essay on where it's going and its effects.

"In your ass," Master rasped with a smirk. Excuse me? "Where!?" I screeched. Master chuckled like the devil he is. "You heard me right, Kitten. In your gorgeous ass," he confirmed.

"No," I denied. Nothing is entering my ass. Not even a pretty string with balls on it. "Is that so Kitten?" Master asked. I nodded. "Sadly,I don't take orders from you," he said. Chuckling softly.

My eyes widened when I felt a cold substance making contact with my skin. Master rubbed it over my rim and watched me.i felt a finger entering my no entry zone. I wiggled in place since I could not close my legs.

Damnit. I mentally yelled in frustration. Master continued pushing the intruding finger further into my ass."Master-," I whined. He finally bottomed and begun pulling it out only to push it inside again.

"Yes, kitten," he said. Mocking my whiny state. 'Stop," I mumbled. But he did not stop. He only when faster. My whines turned into moans at some point.

"Look at that, pup," Master said. I felt shuffling on the bed. "I can see Master. The little brat is enjoying this," Sir replied sounding closer. Sir begun massaging my breasts.

"God,you look so beautiful," Master rasped. That made my back ache off the bed. Suddenly,I clenched around nothing. Master had taken his fingers out of me.

I wanted to cry from all the teasing I've been receiving. Sir continued neading my breasts. "You are not supposed to enjoy this. It's a punishment afterall," Master said with a smirk on his face.

"Pouting won't save you from this, kitten," he said. I didn't not even notice that I was pouting. Sir chuckled . I scowled at him.

The uncomfortable feeling of something probing my rim came back . This time with vengeance. The first ball was small which made it easier to enter. " Good girl," Master praised.

"Relax babe. It would be easier to take them when you are relaxed," Sir said. I took his advice and relaxed. Though that did not stop my heart from try to escape from my chest.

Master pushed the second and the third ball which were not that big. The fourth ball was slightly bigger. Don't get me started on the fifth. The sixth ball was going to split me in half. I was not excited about taking that one.

" Our girl's taking the balls so well, isn't she Master?" Sir asked. Master ignored him and pushed two more balls into my ass. At this point I was moaning in both pain and pleasure. That made no sense to me but nothing made sense when it came to my pleasure.

Sir leaned down and sucked a nipple into his warm mouth. My back ached from the bed. The bed shifted again. Master was on the floor. He put stuff on the bed and continued searching.

He climbed on the bed again. Sir stopped sucking on my boobs and gave Master his attention. God this man are going to kill me with all this teasing.

"Master,do you think she's ready for that?" Sir asked. That did not sit well with me. At all. I head Master chuckle. " Bratty girls can take anything,Pup," he rasped. I wanted to scream that bratty girls can't take anything but I kept shut. God knows how much trouble my mouth got me into.

I took long deep breaths to calm my raging heart. The anticipation of what's coming kept it going. Not slowing down even a little. A leathery material grazed my clit making it throb even more. A moan ripped out of my throat without my permission. I feel betrayed by my own body right now.

I risked glance at Master. He looked pleased. Very pleased. Without any warning, he raised the crop and snapped it on my clit. "Fuck," I screamed. Master smirked and snapped the crop on my clit a few more times. Each time, my screams got louder and louder.

Two fingers were thrusted into my pussy and began moving. The orgasm that ripped through me painfully. I could not stop screaming. Both Master and Sir seemed pleased with everything that took place.

"Good job, Kitten. You took your punishment very well," Master praised. Sir patted my heard. I gave him a shaky smile while catching my breath. "I'll go prepare a bath," Sir suggested._____

I'm finally done with this chapter thank God. I won't apologize for taking that long to update for personal reasons of course. Though I hope you enjoy it and don't forget to give me your feedback and spank that pretty star for me.

The reads have been increasing which motivates me to keep going. I'm very pleased. Very ,very pleased. Thank you again and I love every one of you. Enjoy your holidays my lovelies

-bunny

chapter twenty five

Vivian

I could not move without feeling the outcome of not telling Master what he wanted to know. While they gave me a well deserved bath,I told them everything. "Guess you didn't check the garage," Master mumbled. Sir scowled in response.

"Who hides in a garage anyways," Sir exasperated. Master nuzzled the side of my face and hummed in content. "My smart Kitten. Apparently." He chuckled softly which made me giggle. Sir gave up his scowling contest and patted my head. "Yeah,very smart," he said.

Hiding in that little car was so God damn uncomfortable. I had to suck in a lot to even fit between the seats. When I heard him leaving,relief washed over me. I could finally get out of my hiding place.

His concern over my supposed disappearance made me a little guilty. I did not mean to worry him that bad. It also made my chest tighten with the knowledge that he cared about me that much. My lips tilted in a smile as I continued to wait for customers to come to Mrs Halls.

It has been a few weeks since I saw her. It may seem bizarre but I miss her. I'll make sure to go visit her after work. The door bell rang, signalling the arrival of customers. I quickly got out of my head and focused on making the loud woman more money.

My practiced polite smile made its appearance as I served customer after customer. By the time I was done, my feet already hurt and I could not feel my face. Damn smile broke my muscles. I massaged the feeling back into my cheeks.

The highlight of this horrible day was going back home to my boyfriends. I have not heard much of them the whole day due to having very little breaks. I made quick work of my uniform after preparing the place for tomorrow and made my way to the door.

"Vivian," Lloyd, one of Mrs Halls's newest employee called. I gazed at the door longingly before giving Lloyd my attention. Damn my luck. "Yes," I replied politely. He took quick, determined steps towards me.

"Uh...I was wondering if we could grab some coffee," he said rubbing the back of his neck. The slightest hue of pink touched his cheeks. I almost smiled at how cute he looked. Before I could utter a response, the door opened.

The beautiful yet sinful specimen that walked in had me swallowing. Duncan really was intimidating. I jumped away from Lloyd like I was a kid caught doing something they should have not been doing. Duncan raised a brow at Lloyd before striding towards me.

When he was close enough, he yanked me close to the wall he calls a chest. I had to crane my neck so I could get a look at his face. Annoyance was clearly written on his face while he stared Lloyd straight in the eye.

I too looked at the guy who not too long ago asked me a question I do not answer. I was going to decline his offer but the beast of a man had to walk in just when my mouth remembered its job. I mentally rolled my eyes at my dumb self and sent Lloyd an apology with my eyes.

His snapped towards me for a split second. He nodded. "I guess I'll see you around,"he said before hurrying towards the door like his ass was on fired. I finally gave the annoying man my attention. He was... smiling. It almost looked sweet and innocent. Almost.

"That was no necessary," I mumbled against his chest. He chuckled and put both his arms around me. "Yes it was. He was talking to what belonged to me," he said, tightening his arms around me. I could not breath anymore.

I tapped his chest and wiggled around. He let go of me with a chuckle while I finally could breath. Giant. Compared to him,I probably looked like a tiny doll. The ones you put on keychains. I looked so damn tiny I swear he could break me.

"Get out of your head," he commanded. That snapped me put of it. I shook my head and gave him all my attention. "Let's go home," he said already moving towards the door. I followed behind him and locked up.

I recognised the car he was moving towards as one of the many I saw in his underground garage. It made a sound to signal that it was unlocked. He strode to the passager side and opened the door for me. I would have broken it if it was up to me. Instead of going side way like normal car doors,it went up like a butterfly wing.

Without touching anything,I got inside and it smoothly shut. He got in the driver's side and drove off. It was then that I noticed he's not drive towards their home. "Uh... Duncan," I called. He hummed in response. Glancing at me for a split second before focusing on the road again. "Where are we going," I asked. He did not answer my question instantly.

I have up trying to figure out our destination and looked at him. "It's a surprise," he finally said. I don't like surprises and I know that he knows that. I scowled at him. "No,tell me. Where are we going," I demanded. If I could stomp my foot,I'd also be doing that. He continued staring ahead not sparing me a glance one more time. "Duncan," I whined in annoyance.

He rolled his eyes before turning a corner. Wait,what? I stared at him with my eyes wide open. He chuckled at my expression and turned another corner. This part of the city was ritzy. Expensive looking buildings surrounded us. Everything looked so beautiful. I was in awe of it all.

I had actually forgotten why I was whining until he made a stop infront of yet another beautiful building. There were two man dressed in all black in front of the door. I did not notice Duncan until he was on my side, opening the door. He offered his hand. I stared at it at first.

He cleared his throat, clearly not patient enough for my indecisive brain. I hesitantly took it and got out of the car. Another man appeared out of no where.

We stood before the imposing building. Though I wondered why. Duncan had a far away look in his eyes. I continued staring at him while dealing with my racing thoughts. I wanted to know why we were here and what we are going to do but I kept my mouth shut. He might just spank me right here.

Duncan shook his head, getting back to the here are now. I hummed in question. He looked at me. Those beautiful eyes slapping the walls to my soul out of the way in search of something. His lips twitched in different directions, approving of whatever he saw in my eyes,I assume.

I cleared my throat. Looking at anything but him. A soft pink painted my cheeks. He chuckled before walking towards the man in black guarding the door. They exchanged subtle nods before opening the door for us. "Thank you," I said. They looked at each other for a moment before continuing their scary-man-in-black posture.

"What are we doing here," I asked. My question went unanswered yet again. Like the brat I am...I dropped to the floor. Landing on my ass ungracefully. I yelped in pain. "What are you doing," Duncan asked. I rubbed at my ass, trying to make the pain go away as fast as possible. I too ignored his question and focused on my poor back side.

" I asked you a question, Kitten," he said in a low voice. " So now I'm obligated to answer your questions while mine are left unanswered," I retorted. His minor glared turned deadly in a few seconds. Fuck. A couple passed by us. The fear in the women's eyes portrayed my own. Apparently I have not learnt to not answer back.

You've done it this time Viv.

chapter twenty six

~Duncan~

This girl is really asking for it. I swear. She visibly gulps in fear." Get up," I say in a low tone. She quickly gets up, fear written all over her face. I would be lying if I say I'm not liking that. She looks really small like this. Like I could hold her in both my palms and take her everywhere I want.

I continue walking, expecting her to follow me without me commanding her to. We enter a dark room on the first floor. With the lights turned off, it looks like a void. Completely drenched in darkness. Hiding equipment, some for pleasure, and some for torture. Sweet, glorious torture.

Which is what my bratty Kitten is going to receive. My initial plan was to give her so much pleasure until she bagged me to stop. But no. She had to piss me off. She did so many things wrong tonight. Haven't she learnt that I'm not her Daddy but her Master. Their Master. My word is law and it should not be questioned. I guess it's about time she learnt for good, I say in my head.

I flick the light switch on. I don't have to turn around to see the terrified expression on her face. I can sense it. Feel it rolling off her and straight into my body. That makes a part of me very happy. I step to the side, motioning for her to enter. She does without saying a word. Eyes wide open. I smirk at her. Showing her how excited I am about this.

She stands in the middle of the room. Sweeping her beautiful eyes over the room. Exemining the many equipment. I close and lock the door. When I turn around,I find her adorable eyes on me searching for answers in my own hard orbs. I slowly make my way to a chair in the corner.

I take a sit and heatedly stare at her. I'm sure her panties are in a puddle of juices. Even with the fear written all over her face,I can see the wanton women in them. Waiting for pleasure in any form. Unfortunately she won't be getting any. Not anymore. She brought all this upon herself. She practically begged for it with her bratty attitude.

"Strip," I command. She makes quick work of her clothes. Standing in nothing but her underwear. The colour of the lacy material complementing her beautiful, smooth skin. My eyes make a slow appraisal from her hot pink painted toes to her thighs. I bite my lower lip and continue to the wetness of her panties. I chuckle at the sight.One of her legs move over the other. My eyes quickly find her heated face. Embarrassment written all over it.

"Spread," I command without breaking the eye contact. She may be embarrassed by her already drenched underwear but she sure is brave. Brave enough to look me straight in the eyes as she spread her legs wide enough for me to see how wet she is for me. "Good girl," I praise. Her eyes close as she shuddered.

That reaction almost made me smirk with satisfaction. The knowledge of having such an effect on another person really does things to the brain. I continued to look at the jewel between her legs. All soaked and practically begging to be worshipped. I cut my eyes to her face again . Embarrassment really looks good on my bratty Kitten. Really good. " On your knees baby doll," I commanded. She softly got to her knees and waited for my next command.

Her beautiful eyes were shielded by her half closed lids. I beckoned her with my fingers. Silently telling her to crawl to me. We've been through this situation enough for her to know what I'm saying without me actually saying the words. Except for the part where she openly and shamelessly disobeys me.

She made slow movements towards me. The corners of her entrancing lips stretched with a smile. I just knew that she was planning something devious. And to be honest,I fucking love it when her pretty mind plots against me. It makes it very exciting to punish her.

When she had reached me,she sat all froggy and looked up at me with her adorable eyes. I looking back at her and smirked."I'm sorry Master, please don't punish me," she whispered. I put both my arms on the armrests and leaned towards her. So close that I could feel her breath on my lips.

I stared at her alluring lips before looking her straight into her eyes. My smirk turned evil in a split second. I put my right hand on her bare shoulder. Looking at it like it was the most fascinating thing in the world. I watched it's every move. Slowly trailing from her shoulder to the arc between her shoulder and neck. Her breathing quickened.

"You see, Kitten," I began. Spreading my fingers over her pretty neck. Beautiful and unmarked."If I forgave you for being bratty,you'd always be bratty," I added. Closing my fingers around it and tightening my hold a little. Her lips parted with every breath she took. I planted a soft kisses from her cheek to the corner of her lips. Her eyes closed like she was savoring the feeling of my lips on her skin. I leaned back a little and admired her flustered face. I liked that look on her. Very pretty.

A shrill sounds interrupted my apprehesal of my sweet kitten. Her eyes startled open. My eyes began searching for the source of the sound. Relief and annoyance battle to be the supreme emotion on her face. That's only making me even more pissed because she's breaking yet another rule. That stupid device should have been on silent. "Aren't we on a piss your master spree today," I mumble. Voice full of so much threat.

"I'm so sorry... I'll go put it on silent," she quickly says. Scrambling off her knees. At this point I'm fuming. I sit back and rest my head against the chair. I try by all means to rain in my rage before I make her eternally afraid of me. Sine she likes being praised so much, i wonder how she'd feel knowing she failed to please me. That thought aids in easing some of my rage. I take a few deep breaths and still my expressions.

When I hear her coming back to the corner I was planning to spank her ass and bruise it for weeks. My cold orbs stare into her guilty and terrified ones. I beckon her to come closer to me. She does so without thinking twice. Before she took her previous position, stopped her. " Take a sit on my lap Kitten," I said. Her confused expression said a lot however she did as she was told. I wait for her to comfortably settle herself on my lap.

I put both my arms around her in a comforting manner. A small smile accompanies my warm embrace. A beautiful smile graces her equally beautiful face. She probably thinks I've forgiven her. Pity her. I clear my throat before I deliver the biggest blow to her entire submissive existence.

"I'm going to tell you a story Kitten, " I whisper across her cheek. Breathing her in. She nods. "It's about a very beautiful submissive who didn't please her master." I felt her stiffen as soon as those last words left my lips. I know she can feel my eyes on her since she cast hers downwards. "I don't think I wanna hear that story, Master," she mumbled.

I clear my throat one more time and tell her the story anyways. With every word that came out of my mouth, her expression remains pained.

After telling her the story, i made her stand in front of me like I'm gonna give her another chance to do better. "Get dressed. We are leaving," I said straightening my own clothes and adjusting myself. When we left the place, she was a spitting image of the perfect sub. With her eyes cast down, not missing a step.

Chapter Twenty seven

~Vivian~

The drive home seemed longer than the drive to that club. Saying my mind is all over the place is an understatement. The story that master told me literally broke my heart. It really hurts knowing that I've disappointed him so much. "She failed to please her master and was deemed a failure ." Those words ring in my head over and over again getting louder each time.

I glance at Duncan for a moment. I know he can see me looking and I want him to see how hurt I am. Why am I feeling this way? Why do I want his forgiveness so much? More questions haunt me the more I look at him. I decide that's only making me feel worse then opt for looking out the window.

The area begins to become familiar as we near home. His and Sir's. I live there too but I don't deserve to. I failed to please him. I failed the only responsibility I had in this house. The wetness in my eyes builds the closer we get to home. Home. Sir's car is packed neatly outside. He was the one calling me earlier. I hung up on him before I even saw who it was.

Duncan packs his car beside Sir's. I quickly open my door before he could do it for me. I feel so weak right now but he doesn't have to see that. He doesn't have to see me cry. Again. I make my way to the door. I can hear Sir singing inside. He's probably making dinner. I open the door and rush past the kitchen so he doesn't see my face. "Hey, why did you disconnect the call..."I sprint to my room before he finished what he was saying.

As soon as the door to my room closes, the water works begin. I'm so confused right now. My feelings are...so confusing. I could head distant murmers from the other room. I continue to cry my confused out as i plot ways to make things better. Better to being a good girls.

At this moment my praise kink has become my worst enemy. It had also become my source of motivation. A big pile of contradiction if you ask me but that's that. As my brain continues to plot, someone softly knocks on the door I've slid down on. My brain screams at me to keep quit and the person would eventually go away.

Does my heart listen? Nope. The confused jit convinces me that this is my opportunity to rectify myself. Am i convinced? Most definitely because i find myself righting myself before i open the door. My daddy is the person behind my door. The feeling of disappointment takes residence in my heart.

My hopes slowly die as i look him over. He also looks disappointed... Guilty. " Can i come in?" he asks. Which i found rather... Confusing. Everything is confusing me today. I nod and step aside. Usually he'd just budge in and make demands like the pain he is. I internally tisk myself for thinking that my Daddy is a pain. He'd have my ass over his knee if he knew.

"I'm sorry," he says as soon as his ass is on my bed. I look at him like he grew a second head. He takes note of my questioning look and nods. Probably to himself because I'm lost. "I'm the person who called you," he finally elaborates. That jerks me out of my confused state and tears sting my already tear wracked eyes.

He stands to come closer to me and i close the reast of the distance. Sobs wreck my body as my pride shakes its head at me. I borrow deeper into his chest as i mentally flip my pride off. He is the cause of the wreckage inside me after all. Its only fair that he be the one to comfort me.

I'll kill him later for this though, as i plot some more.

Chapter twenty eight

Sir-

I pull her closer to me as she continues to sob into my chest. I wonder what happened between her and Master. Matter of fact, where were they? That is my reason for calling her in the first place. I wanted to know what I should make for dinner and when she would get back. "Hey," I whisper against her forehead. She continues to sob as if I did not say a thing.

I gently pull her away from my chest and slowly lift her chin. Her eyes are closed probably shielding her beautiful wet brown orbs from me. That actually rubs me off the wrong way. "hey" I whisper again. Her eyeball moves inside her closed lids. I softly kiss her left lid then her right. The soft sigh that leaves her lips gives me the green flag to continue peppering kissed in random places on her face.

"I fucked up", she whispers loud enough fir her words to reach my ears. With my face inches away from hers, I blow light air on her face for her to continue talking. She tells me about where they were and everything that happened. At some point she began crying again while explaining. I feel like the world's biggest asshole for calling her. She could have redeemed herself and finished her task if I didn't call.

"I'm so sorry," I say pulling her back to my chest. She sighed heavily and borrowed deeper into my chest. Then I remembered that I am Duncan's submissive. That I've been his sub for years and I have also gone through what she's experiencing right now. My chest aches from just thinking about it. And then it aches some more for Vivian and because that I might be the reason for it. My arms tighten around my sweet baby girl and sigh.

However, I have a plan on how to get back on good terms with master. I'm scared that she is not going to like it one bit. With how long I have been Duncan's sub, you'd think I'm used to his punishments. The answer is yes but that does not mean that I have gotten immune to the intensity. At times I also find myself near tears with how intense he is. Even when he's not making me pay for something I did wrong intentionally.

"I have a plan, but you are not going to like it" I tell her. She pulls away from my chest and looks me straight in the eyes. Her determination tells me that she's past caring about her likes and dislikes. She waits patiently for me to continue talking. I guess master taught her witty little mouth patience. I smile to myself and pet her like the sweet kitten she is. She aches a questioning brow at me, and I cough to hide the chuckle that almost escaped the confines of my throat.

"As much as I like your determination towards pleasing master, I'm afraid you really need to think clearly about what I'm about to tell you." She gives me a nod and continue staring at me. We go over the plan a few times in her room. That evening she ate dinner in her room while I was face to face with Duncan's sour mood. I'm lucky I did not get railed that night as a way to release his emotions.

Chapter twenty nine

Duncan-

The wonderful thing about being a Master is allowing your senses to take control to avoid mistakes during scenes. I had a feeling that they were plotting against. When we got back, Vivian ran inside the house before I could talk to her. When I got inside, Sir asked me to look after the food while he went to speak to her. She did not even come to the dinner table. That made me very suspicious of the man I've been living with for years. The mood in the bedroom was also kind of tense. I can take the blame for that.

Regardless of how tired I was, I woke up way too early and made us breakfast. Sir woke up when I was done cooking. A low good morning left his lips while he was rubbing the sleep out of his eyes. He sat on the other side of the counter and ran his eyes over everything I have prepared. "No work today?" I shook my head and continued looking at him. I needed to know what schemes he and our little kitten were up to. Unfortunately, he is a switch which means ill ever get a clue when he wants me to have one. I silently sighed and dished up for him and myself.

However, his eyes have been too low for me to get a glimpse of what is going on behind them. A very smart move on his part. Which means I'm only left with one person to give me clues. We ate our breakfast in silence as well. It did not sit well with me how bothered I was with the lack of conversation. It really unusual of me. Sir cleared his throat more times than I've heard him clear it. This was unlike us. Usually, he would be telling me something stupid one of his friends did or about his project and we would go over them.

Ever since she moved in our whole dynamic changed. You can say that she changed us in a way. If we are not discussing school, work, or nothings, we are discussing her. As is she's sensing that I'm thinking about her, her bedroom door slowly opens. One thing bout our kitten is that she loves food and absolutely nothing can come between her and food. Her small foot falls on the floor slowly make their way towards the kitchen.

Her curly mess of hair is the first thing we see as she peeks around the corner that leads to the kitchen. Our eyes connect as soon as hers reach me because I wanted to see what she was going to do. The windows to her soul always betray her making it easier to read her. I can say that they are the source of her downfall when it comes to me. The war continues for a bit longer before she took a deep breath, and the rest of her body came into view.

With her eyes cast low enough for me to be robbed of their beauty, she made her way to the stove. "Good morning baby," Sir drawled while eyeing me with a smirk. That actually confuses me because I really don't know why he's smirking. It's understandable that she is hiding from me. It finally clicked that I was suspicious of a plotting switch and submissive. I shutdown my expressions to avoid giving myself away. I took the last sip of my coffee and stood up to take my dishes to the sink.

She hummed her greeting back and continued dishing up for herself. I rinsed my dishes and made my way towards her. She is my submissive yes, but I want a relationship with her outside the one we already established. Her body stiffened when I placed my hands on her hips. I front touched her back as I came closer to her. Her small body fit perfectly against my much larger one. I put my nose on the spot between her neck and shoulder and slowly peppered the area with light kisses. I felt a little bit of the tension leave her body.

"Good morning baby girl, "I whispered against her neck. I felt my words travel through her body in the form of a shiver that she tried to hide. I smirked against her now heated skin before snaking my arms around her. I don't know if she leaned against me on purpose or by mistake, but my body loved the feel of her. I trailed open mouthed kisses from her neck to her ear and said," I'm sorry kitten." Those aren't the words that I really wanted to say but the way her body completely relaxed against me made the word vomit worth it.

I could feel the wheels turning from my position behind her. She took a deep breath before she turned in arms to face me. Her eyes were so beautiful, filled with so many confusing emotions...And hope. She took yet another breath, this one was to probably try to slow down the pace of her heartbeat. " Why are you apologizing Duncan?" I loved that she used my name instead of my title. I leaned forward and kissed her forehead as a reward.

Her eyes were shut when I leaned back to look at her face. My brain is screaming at me to not do this, but my heart is on a different path. "I'm sorry about yesterday, "I whispered loud enough for everyone in the room to hear. I can feel the incredulous look Sir was giving me. I could feel it penetrate my skin and grab my heart in a vise for my brain. I could feel the accusation in just that look for the hard time I gave him during his training but now I'm even apologizing to this beautiful kitten.

Sir was not the only one was shocked about my apology to Vivian. her eyes were open so wide like she was a deer in head lights. I wanted to laugh at how comical they both looked but the matter required a man as close to their Master as possible. " I should have not told you that story. It was completely made up." It was like the more words spilled out of my mouth the more she went into shock.

My view of her beautiful orbs was taken away when they shut for a moment. I waited patiently for her to digest my words before she could give me her answer. A tear escaped under her lid and soon after more followed. I pulled her towards my chest, offering her the comfort i new i should have given her last night. I sighed into her hair and tightened my arms around her as her silent sobs wrecked her body.

The whole time Sir silently observed our exchange like a hawk watching over its next prey. I wonder what his devious mind is plotting. The emotional girl in my arms took a calming deep breath and put her arms around me. I also need to apologize to Sir but that would be over doing it and he knows it. It is another reason why he is so quiet. Observing with a wicked grin on his beautiful face just like our kitten.

She leans back and looks me straight in the eyes. it was like she was bagging me to do something besides give her the comfort I owe her. My ego was inflated so high that it wouldn't come down for days. I ran my fingers over her tear-stained cheek and chuckled. She was shaping up to be such a good submissive. faster than Sir but it's completely understandable because he is a switch.

I brought my face closer to hers and planted a soft kiss on the corner of her cheek to the corner of her lips moving on to her other cheek. I heard shuffling behind me which split my attention between two of my subs. Sir came closer to us, standing close enough to Vivian to deliver soft kisses on her shoulder. one of his hands brushed my arm which sent some blood straight to my dick. that made me dive towards Vivians lips like my next breath was between her lips.

We worked together to get our sub all hot and bothered. It did not matter that her hands were all over us. Usually, we would have had them tied somewhere or held against something depending on the location. It felt like we needed to be touched as much as she wanted to touch us. The mission was to get her bagging and screaming for the neighbors to complain and seemed like Sir agreed.

While Sir focused on driving her crazy with need with hungry kisses and both of his hands on her tits, I slowly made my way towards her lower part. Leaving open mouthed kisses all over her exposed legs, nipping her and there. I kissed her everywhere but the place I knew that she wanted me the most. By the looks of it she did not appreciate my that at all. her hips moved in a seeking motion for my lips, I chuckled and slapped her on the side of her thigh. A startled breath left her lips which fueled me to give her another one on her other thigh.

Sir glanced at me and nodded for me to give her what she wanted. As much as I did not appreciate that I shoved my annoyance at the back of my head and zeroed in on her cunt. if she was not wearing any panties with her shorts, the wet spot on her shorts wouldn't be that small. i took a whiff at her scent and allowed it to drive me insane with need. more blood rushed to my dick as I ran my nose over the wet spot on her shorts. I gripped her hips to push her clit against my nose which made her gasp away from Sir's lips.

"The next time you stop kissing me, I'm gonna put something productive in your mouth, "he warned. She quickly apologised and crushed her lips against Sir's. He groaned in approval and shoved his hand in her hair to keep her in place while he devoured her. I gave the wet spot I helped her responsive cunt make. I smile and slowly push her shorts and panties down her legs in unison. She kicked them away for me the rest of the way, probably eager for my mouth on her pussy.

She was practically dripping with how wet she was for us, my mouth wanted to taste her so bad. And that's what I did. I dove in like a mad man on a hunt for immortality, hungry and relentless. The sweetest whimpers left her mouth which was still in lip lock with Sir's. I put one of her legs over my shoulder to get a much more comfortable angle of her delicious cunt. That seemed to do it for her as her hips battled with offering more of her cunt to me and shying away from my tongue on her clit.

I put my hand on the leg that was over my shoulder and forced her to take my tongue while my other hand was rubbing circles around her dripping entrance. That's when she started to moan like her life depended on the sounds that escaped her lips. My eyes went to where they were connected, wanting to see if he'd put something productive like he warned. Sadly, my sweet Puppy was in a trance like it was the first time his ears were being blessed by the sounds she was making.

I mentally rolled my eyes at him and shoved two fingers into my Kitten's pussy. Her walls gripped my fingers in a vise while the tell tales of an orgasm ripped through her. I found Sir's eyes on me, and I blinked once to tell him not to allow her to orgasm without permission. the look in eyes changed as he gripped her jaw a bit forcefully. Her head rose to look at him. at that point I wanted to see her, I wanted her to look at me and show me how good I was making her feel. Unfortunately, I can't have her pussy and her eyes on the same level.

"You aren't allowed to come yet," he said loud enough for me to hear over her loud moans. I moved my fingers so abruptly that a scream was torn from her throat. That caught us off guard a bit which made me pause. Her loud scream reduced to soft whimpers and beautiful begging eyes. But only one thing was left to be one, she only had to beg loud and proud. she knew what she had to do by the looks of the movement of her head. She knew it and she refused to give us what we want, what we craved.

I moved my fingers slow at first to give her time to adjust and she gifted us with whimpers so soft they sounded like a purring kitten. She knew that if she came without permission the punishment will not be as easy as prolonging an orgasm. While my fingers worked her to the brink of insanity, Sir was busy whispering sweet nothings into her ear. Together we worked towards driving her to the ends of the world with over stimulation.

Her soft whimpers turned into pleas and screams that I assumed the neighbors could hear by now. I lowered my lips to the bundle of sensitive nerves between her glistering lips. Her hips battled between giving me more of her and pushing me away. It was honestly entertaining, watching her coming undone before us. It filled me with so much pride watching her give herself to us, trusting us enough to allow us to make her scream.

I pulled my head back and gave Sir the go ahead to allow her to release everything she has been holding back. I could see that he was enjoying her torture way too much for him to give me that look. A look that told me that I have created a watered-down vision of myself, a sadist. " Look at me," her whispered against her neck. Her eyes were scrunched closed, probably to focus more on not releasing without permission. her eyes slowly opened, dazed with torturous pleasure. "Look at you being such a good girl, hovering over the edge. "He kissed the corner of her slightly opened lips.

She whimpered in response, too wrung out to formulate proper words. Sir leaned back to ravel in the beauty that she was now that we have thoroughly edged her. It was not the plan but it was a good way to start a morning for all of us. he nodded, signaling that she can let go. I felt the telltales of a violent orgasm. My fingers moved faster on their own accord. Her walls began to spasm around my fingers, making me reduce the speed of my fingers. All of a sudden, liquid gushed everywhere as she violently shook.

My clothes and parts of the floor were drenched with her, my face was no different. I licked the moisture on my lips, sampling. before she could calm down completely, I went in for the kill, latching onto her pussy and licking her clean. A second orgasm wreaked havoc her body while I finished cleaning her up with my toung. A second sensation of something wet fall on my shoulder. I leaned back and missed the last ribbon of come from the direction of an angry fisting. It was not my first time feeling his come on me but it was the first he had literally came on me. I honestly did not know how to feel about that but stare at him.

All I knew is that he was going to pay for it.

chapter thirty

Sir

The next following days moved on smoothly with the gloomy cloud above my head. to be honest my aim was not to come on him. However, it filled me with immense pleasure to see him covered in my come.

I knew the day that he was going to make me pay for my mistake will come and it was not going to be a nice one. I imagine him wringing orgasm after orgasm after orgasm out of me. He might just resolve to edging with a cock ring or make me watch him fuck Vivian with a vibrator inside me.

Brainstorming my punishments filled me with so much anticipation and fear at the same time. One thing I have learnt about Duncan is that he can be unpredictable as fuck. He cannot be confined to one narrative when it comes to the way his mind works which leaves room for a lot of fear.

It was Wednesday and I had no class, but I had a meeting with my friends later on. they were supposed to come over to the house but their fear of my scary dad looking boyfriend always wins. A door opening pulled me out of my wonderous thoughts. It was Duncan.

So far we have slept next to each other with the occasional visit from Vivian, but we have not discussed what happened. I can see him stew in his own plots at times when he looks at me. When I look at him with questioning eyes, he continues staring for a while then looks away.

I wonder what he was doing home so early. when he rounded the corner, our eyes connected with so many things that need to be said but never left the lips. I looked away, feigning indifference which was a bad idea by the sound of his low growl.

" I'm still shocked to this day that you literally came on me,". I continued feigning indefereence like i haven't heard him talk. Being complicent brings so much satisfaction but nothing beats riling your dom up. People might be suprised at the things adrenaline can get you into.

Currently I am planting a seed. A dangerous seed and God help me I can't wait for the fruits. I glance at him at the corner of my eye. I could literally see his patience running thin which meant that I was really close to getting what I want. two parts within me were warring against each other. one fighting for myself preservation, to avoid pissing him off as much as possible. the masochistic part of me wanted him to put me on all fours and fuck me into my place. make him make wish I listened to the more rational part of myself.

That just filled me with more anticipation than I can handle. I was practically buzzing in my sit for what's to come. He crept closer to me until he was behind me practically breathing down my neck. "You know I am very fond of your disrespect," he said, running a hand from my arm slowly to my shoulder. His words sent an excited thrill down my spine." It reminds me of all the lessons I need to teach you again. Keeps things between us so interesting." All most there. The masochistic voice in my heard whispered.

His words settled somewhere deep in me like a cold that never wanted to go away. I took deep breaths to calm my already racing heart. This is what

I lived for, passion that has my heart racing like I am about to jump off a mountain. It got me to understand why people actually did it. " You don't say," I lamely uttered, digging my grave a bit deeper.

One of his hands collared my neck so softly. Just that touch put me in a space where only he existed. Where he was and is my only source of oxygen. The collar wasn't tight but it's significance added more miles for my already racing heart. I swallowed the saliva that has been collecting in my mouth.

He tipped my head back so i could get a good look at his pretty face. I wanna ride it. The creepy voice in my head whispered. I didn't disagree with it at all. I wanted to do exactly that so bad that my underwear probably had a wet spot. "You know what keeps me asleep at night with dreams so beautiful, it's almost hard to wake up?" he breathed against my hair rhetorically. I tried twice as hard to take controlled breaths before i passed out. "The fact that i can fuck both you and Vivian so thoroughly that ya'll beg for more".

The truthfulness of that statement had me clutching my fists. He does make us beg for more and we love it. That thought alone should have bothered me but i only got excited.

www.ingramcontent.com/pod-product-compliance
Lightning Source LLC
Chambersburg PA
CBHW072212070526
44585CB00015B/1301